REGISTER THIS BOOK NOW!

Access the *DO OR DIE* Online Portal
& Receive Additional *FREE* Resources

Just Go To:

www.DOorDIEthebook.com

Once you have registered the book, you immediately will be redirected into the online portal that features a wide variety of valuable supplemental materials, tools and business-building information:

- ➤ The Author's "Million Dollar Rolodex" Resource List
- ➤ "The Seven Agency Success Factors" Overview
- ➤ "Defined Contribution: Revolution for EB Agencies" Audio Seminar
- ➤ "Plug Your Agency's Marketing Drain" Webinar
- ➤ "Five Steps to Prospecting" Cheat Sheet
- ➤ "Brokers' Top 7 Time Wasters" Audio Seminar
- ➤ "30-Day Agency Marketing Guide" Special Report
- ➤ "Four Steps to Consultative Selling" Webinar
- ➤ "Selling with Questions" Audio Seminar
- ➤ "Five Fatal Mistakes Cross-Selling Voluntary" Cheat Sheet
- ➤ "Opportunity Is Knocking...Do You Hear It?!" Webinar

And much more....

Plus, we'll frequently update this online portal for your benefit.

You'll also discover more information about a very powerful program for elite agency principals that will empower you to apply the agency rein-vention strategies in this book much more easily, more effectively and faster than you could on your own.

We look forward to receiving your feedback about this book, and know that it as well as the online resources will serve you and your benefits agency very well!

You Don't Need to Read This Book

If you are an agency leader, the reason you're holding this book in your hands is because you want your agency to survive Obamacare and thrive in the post-reform world.

While this book is a step-by-step guide to agency reinvention, there is another way, an alternative method, to go about not only gaining the knowledge you need but also to actually apply and implement the strategies effectively and efficiently in your agency.

In the final chapter of this book, Chapter 21, we detail this "alternative method" that will deliver your firm the desired results far more easily and faster than you could get by just reading this book and then trying to apply the strategies and tactics on your own.

In short, this alternative is a highly intensive and intentional program for agency leaders who want to move quickly and accurately by leveraging the success, mistakes and wisdom of other top benefits agency leaders for their own business's reinvention.

Thus, if you so desire, you can choose to skip the bulk of this highly informative and eye-opening treatise, and simply learn about this program, determine if it's for you and your agency and then actively participate in the program if you are accepted into it.

Of course you should know, if you do participate in this program, we will ask you to...yep, you guessed it...**read the book!**

To Debi Poczatko —
with warmest regards,

Boom!

10/29/14

Nelson Griswold

DO OR DIE

Reinventing Your Benefits Agency for Post-Reform Success

A Step-By-Step Guide for Agency Leaders

Nelson L. Griswold

with Scott Cantrell

HIGH
ROI
PRESS

Advisory Selling™, Sales Triangle™, Cross-Sell Solutions System™, Broker Boot Camp™, 21st Century Agency™, and High-ROI Marketing™ are all registered trademarks of Bottom Line Solutions, Inc.

Published by High-ROI Press
115 Penn Warren Dr., Suite 300-304
Brentwood, TN 370276
(615) 656-5974
Fax: (866) 489-5632

Griswold, Nelson L. III, 1959–
    DO or DIE: Reinventing Your Benefits Agency for Post-Reform Success / Nelson L. Griswold, with Scott Cantrell
        p.cm.
    Includes index.
    1. Business. 1. Title
        ISBN 978-0-9882823-0-8

Printed and bound in the United States of America

This book is dedicated to Petric, who was generous enough to teach me the right way to sell, and to all the agency leaders across the country who have asked us for help to survive and thrive post reform.

Acknowledgements

I first want to thank Scott Cantrell – my friend, business partner and marketing genius – whose contributions to this book are innumerable. Not only did Scott contribute all the key concepts on marketing, he provided me with the rough draft for the section on 21ˢᵗ Century Marketing. And he is a fantastic sounding board, as well. Moreover, it was Scott who encouraged me to turn a series of articles on agency reinvention into a book. Thanks, buddy. You did yeoman's work...this book is as much yours as it is mine.

On behalf of Scott and myself, I also want to thank the great folks at *Employee Benefit Adviser* magazine, who gave me a monthly column and, thus, got me writing on some of the topics now in this book. As mentioned, the nucleus and inspiration for this book was a five-part series I wrote for my *EBA* column. A special thank you to Jim Callan, Jim McLaughlin, Elizabeth Galentine and Dave Albertson. I appreciate your friendship and the opportunity to work with such fine professionals.

Sincere thanks go to my friend and colleague Walt Podgurski of the Workplace Benefits Association, who has been very kind and supportive of me. His example as a creative and successful entrepreneur in this industry has been a great inspiration.

I owe a debt of gratitude to one of the industry's premier thought leaders, Ron Leopold, who was generous and kind enough to write the Foreword to this book. The book is much the better for it.

Because they are such a fantastic resource and support, I want to thank the members of my weekly Entrepreneurs Mastermind Group – Jason, Shank, Gary, Jacob, Brian and Scott. Thanks, guys, for keeping me energized and accountable.

Finally, I want to thank my family, Mom, Dad, my brother Johnny, and especially my patient and wonderful wife, Elizabeth, and my two great kids, Maggie and Bo, for their support and for putting up with the craziness around getting this project done. I love you all so much!

—Nelson L. Griswold

About the Authors

Nelson L. Griswold

Nelson Griswold is one of the insurance industry's leading experts on agency growth and a recognized authority on workplace voluntary benefits (WVB), consultative selling and cross-selling.

He serves as Managing Director of the Agency Growth Mastermind Network, an executive peer-exchange program for benefits agency owners.

Formerly a senior executive and top producer at a national benefits communication and enrollment firm, Nelson founded Bottom Line Solutions, Inc., a full-service sales & marketing consulting firm, to provide the insurance industry with proven growth strategies. He and his firm consult with agencies across the country to help them increase their revenues and market penetration with voluntary benefits and high-ROI sales & marketing systems.

He has trained numerous carrier sales teams and thousands of producers to cross-sell WVB effectively with his Broker Boot Camp® workshops using his Cross-Sell Solutions System® that was featured in *Benefit Selling* magazine.

A Contributing Editor and monthly columnist for *Employer Benefit Adviser* magazine, Nelson is regularly published in other leading industry publications and is an in-demand keynoter speaker and presenter at industry events. He serves on the board of the Workplace Benefits Association.

He and his wife live in Nashville.

Scott Cantrell

Scott Cantrell is one of the insurance industry's leading marketing strategists and serves as Director of the Agency Growth Mastermind Network.

A top expert in direct marketing strategies for insurance, he provides agency clients with high-ROI marketing strategies that can be held accountable for results.

Scott has a rich background as a professional communicator, trainer, and strategic marketer. Before focusing exclusively on the insurance industry, he worked for years as an independent consultant across industries, taking the best practices from one industry and successfully applying them in others.

A frequent speaker and keynote presenter at industry events, Scott writes for leading industry publications including *Employee Benefit Adviser*, *Producers eSource* and *Canadian Insurance Top Broker*.

He lives in Nashville.

Contents

Foreword by Ron Leopold   v

Prologue – Two Men's Journeys to the Summit   1

Introduction   7

ONE   **Danger, Chaos & Opportunity**   15
The Clock Is Ticking... And Why It Doesn't Matter   23
Opportunity Is Knocking...Do You Hear It?   29
Touring A 21st Century Agency   39
Four Steps to Become a 21st Century Agency   47

TWO   **21st Century Portfolio**   53
New Toolbox of Solutions   59
Putting Wellness in Your Toolbox   69
The Voluntary Toolbox   75

THREE   **21st Century Marketing**   85
Six Marketing Concepts   91
Plug the Marketing Drain   101
The Marketing Success Equation   111
20 Strategies, Tactics & Tools   117

FOUR   **21st Century Selling**   131
From Transactional to Consultative Selling   135
The Sales Triangle   143
It's Not What You Sell, It's How   149
Four Steps to Advisory Selling   157

FIVE   21st Century Management   **167**

Agency Management Strategies   173

Sales Management   181

Keeping Score in Your Benefits Agency   189

SIX   Putting It All Together in Your Agency   **201**

Evaluate Your Current Agency Situation   207

Develop A Timeline for Your Climb   215

Take Your Next Step   227

Contact Information   **233**

Appendix   **235**

It is not necessary to change; survival is not mandatory."
—W. Edwards Deming

Foreword

In the last two years I've had the opportunity to present to large gatherings of brokers and consultants on the subject of health care reform. Orange County, CA. Minneapolis. Philadelphia. Denver. Tampa.

Predictably, PPACA has been a huge draw for these gatherings of intermediaries. Throughout the various stages of the roller coaster ride that all of us have experienced around this legislation, everyone in our industry has been asking "What does this mean to us?" "What does this mean to me?" Fair enough.

What always struck me, however, was that broker audiences seemed to be divided into two camps: those that took a "This is going to be big and we're going to have to adapt" position; and those that took the position "How can they do this to us?"

Proto-adaptors and *Brokersauruses.*

If you're a broker or consultant and you think that that PPACA is all about you ("How can they do this to us!?!?") ...this may be "the conclusion of your broadcast day." Turn off your black & white television and go back to bed. Or, read this book with a VERY open mind. It's time to reboot.

At MetLife, we recently fielded a comprehensive survey of brokers and consultants in the post health care reform age. What we found was that brokers and consultants have moved far beyond a "wait and see" attitude and are taking action. They are considering a wide variety of initiatives to help solve their clients' needs and, at the same time, increase the overall profitability and sustainability of their firms. In short, what we found was that intermediaries are starting to look to the very solutions described in this book.

When asked, more than 80 percent of brokers and consultants expected their clients to rely on them even more three years from now than they do today. That's good news. Great news. The majority of these intermediaries are considering new models and strategies in order to grow their businesses. Most popular strategies include enhancing consultant services, selling more voluntary products, and becoming more involved in health and wellness programs. According to the MetLife study, voluntary disability coverage, life insurance, and dental are expected to become more important to their firm's profitability over the next three years. More brokers and consultants were taking it a step further by adding non-traditional voluntary product options such as auto and home insurance, vision care and legal services.

The migration from commission-based practices to fee-based ones was one of the more telling (if not predictable) findings in the study. Fee-based consulting services, particularly those focused on helping clients with benefit and cost-management solutions, have become more popular among today's brokers and consultants both as an innovative and defensive growth strategy in light of legislative pressures forcing commission-based services to decline. Approximately 75 percent of all respondents predict that they will spend more time with clients on strategic and value-based consulting services three years from now, post healthcare reform.

Linking employee benefits and group coverages to the business fundamentals of your clients – employee tenure and retention, employee recruitment and attraction, and worker productivity and engagement – is where the successful broker of tomorrow will focus. Nelson alludes to it repeatedly: Look up from your spreadsheets. Shopping rates is table stakes. Talking credible and legitimate business value is where the new action lies.

It is interesting to note that while 97 percent of brokers and consultants report that they have worked to keep their clients up to speed on health care reform developments, only 21 percent of employers say they are very satisfied with the information they are receiving. In large part this difference may be because of unrealistic client expectations – many answers they want simply don't yet exist. Still, brokers and consultants have opportunities to continue to hone their client communication strategies to reflect specific client concerns, frequently asked questions, and information gaps. Improved client understanding and satisfaction will come from providing targeted and customized advice and guidance for specific business situations and questions as they arise.

In addition to traditional benefits, brokers and consultants are recognizing the opportunity for greater involvement, across all sizes of companies, in health and wellness programs and are considering this a growing area:

58 percent of brokers and consultants with clients with 1,000+ employees, and 44 percent of those who primarily work with small/mid-size companies (less than 1,000 employees).

By creating meaningful incentives and opportunities to promote healthy behaviors, these programs are now broadly accepted as a way to help control company health care expense – in fact, 72 percent of employers who offer such programs say they are effective at reducing costs.

In short, the MetLife study sets the stage for the need for a book like the one Nelson Griswold has written.

Like Nelson, I believe that there is a great deal of important work that needs to get done.

Like Nelson, I believe that health care reform creates more opportunities than obstacles for those of us in the "advise business."

Like Nelson, I believe that (broker and consultant) success in the future will depend largely on the topics addressed in this book.

And like Nelson, I believe that the "trusted advisor" role that the targeted readers of this book embrace is the key to a true renaissance in our business. That is, if you're willing to think differently.

Is there any doubt that how we do business, how we communicate with one another is already changing radically? The truth: group insurance brokers (as a whole) are woefully behind the times when it comes to leveraging technology in business and communication.

It's not just about Twitter. It's not just about LinkedIn. Or Angry Birds. Or the next smart app that will eventually do half of what you used to spend most of the time doing in the blink of an eye. It is about knowing how and when to incorporate new strategies into how you do your business. It's also about recognizing where the revolutionary opportunities lie.

On LinkedIn there is a group entitled "Brokers Who Get Wellness."

If your reaction is: "What's LinkedIn?" better start being a student of new communications technology. Fast.

If your reaction is: "Why should a broker care about wellness?" better reexamine what you do for a living.

If your reaction is: "My employer clients want wellness solutions but I'm not sure how to fit that in to what I do," this book was written for you.

This book is a call to action.

This book is a little bit "growing your group insurance brokerage practice for dummies." And that's quite alright.

This book is a "How To" for brokers and consultants. It is a treasure trove of ideas and strategies.

I have known Nelson Griswold for nearly a decade. I know him to be a true champion of change. Not change for change's sake. He is a business professional with a keen eye for when, where and why change is necessary.

In this book, he makes a strong case for the need to change. He also offers the reader a veritable blueprint for how to make that change happen. What's in this book should be a welcomed message for those of you thinking about your professional future.

I like Nelson Griswold's style of writing. Truth is, I'm not a reader's reader. This book goes down easy. It is conversational and thoughtful. It is a compendium of smart tactics and strategies for large and small brokers to revitalize their business.

Grandpa Simpson from *The Simpsons* (to quote the classics...) put it best:

> *I used to be with it, then they changed what "it" was. Now what was "it" isn't, and what "it" is, is weird and scary. It'll happen to you too.*

Don't let it happen to you. Savor this book.

—**Ronald S. Leopold**, MD, MBA, MPH
Author, MetLife's *2011 Broker and Consultant Study*
Fmr. Vice President & National Medical Director, MetLife
www.ronleopold.com

Everest for me, and I believe for the world,
is the physical and symbolic manifestation of
overcoming odds to achieve a dream.
—Tom Whittaker

What we can do now is contribute to a clearer
understanding of what happened that day on
Everest in the hope that the lessons to be learned
will reduce the risk for others who, like us, take
on the challenge of the mountains.
—Anatoli Boukreev

Prologue

Two Men's Journeys to the Summit

In the mid-1900s, 19 years apart, two courageous adventurers pitted their indomitable spirit against one of the world's most dangerous and daunting challenges...climbing to the summit of Mt. Everest.

One man climbed as part of a well-equipped and well-guided team; one man climbed alone.

Almost two decades before Edmund Hillary made his climb, Maurice Wilson, a former British Army captain and decorated war hero, set himself against the towering peak, determined to become the first man to the top.

These are their stories.[1,2]

Unconquerable Everest

Straddling Nepal and Tibet in the Himalayas, Everest is the world's highest mountain at over 29,000 feet, soaring five and a half miles to the cruising altitude of jetliners and boasting some of the most treacherous terrain on earth. The summit of Everest is the highest point on earth.

Until the late 1800s, the idea of climbing to Everest's summit was considered just a foolhardy dream until a leading English climber gave the idea credence in his 1885 book by suggesting that it was possible.

It wasn't until 1921, however, that a British climber became the first Westerner to ever step foot on Everest, as part of the first British exploratory expedition to reconnoiter and map a route to the summit. Their creation of these maps was a pre-condition for the first full-scale attempt on the Everest the following year.

---

[1] Unsworth, Walt (2000). *Everest – The Mountaineering History* (3rd edition ed.). Bâton Wicks.
[2] Hillary, Edmund (2003), *High Adventure: The True Story of the First Ascent of Everest.* Oxford Univ. Press.

Using these detailed maps, in 1922 a well-equipped British expedition of 160 men, including many Nepalese and Tibetan porters to transport the equipment, initiated the first attempted to climb Everest. From Base Camp at the foot of the mountain, climbers established Camp I at 17,720 ft., then Camp II, an Advanced Base Camp known as Camp III and Camp IV, each at increasingly higher altitudes as they followed the map up the mountain, eventually erecting Camp V at 24,934 ft. Although this expedition didn't reach the summit, these camps became critical milestones for future Everest climbers.

Route with Camps to the Summit of Mt. Everest

To their credit, the British leadership of this 1922 expedition quickly recognized the incalculable value of the native Sherpas, a Nepalese ethnic group, who had proven themselves to be elite mountaineers and experts in mountainous terrain. Subsequent British expeditions promoted some Sherpas from the role of porter to guide.

Between 1922 and 1933, in total three large, well-funded British expeditions tried and failed to reach the summit, although each, using the map created by the previous team, climbed successively higher on the mountain and established higher-altitude camps.

Maurice Wilson and his solo Everest climb

In 1933, inspired by news stories of these earlier British expeditions, Englishman Maurice Wilson decided that he would become the first man to climb Everest. His approach to this monumental challenge was curious, at best.

He had no mountaineering experience, yet his only training was to spend five weeks walking the slight hills of England's Lake District.

Maurice Wilson, 1934

Then, he chose not to learn any technical mountaineering skills or to buy any specialist climbing equipment. Most incredibly, he chose to make the attempt alone, without a team of climbers or guides. But perhaps most critical, he lacked maps from the earlier expeditions of the routes up the mountain and camp milestones.

In 1934, Wilson arrived in Tibet, stopping at a Buddhist monastery at the base of Everest. As he prepared to start his climb up the mountain, the depth of his naïveté was revealed when he turned down the offer of help from three Sherpas who had been porters on the 1933 British Everest expedition. He also refused to take any of the climbing equipment left behind by the 1933 expedition.

On April 16, he continued his climb up Mt. Everest alone. This first journey was an almost comical false start during which he kept getting lost and was repeatedly forced to retrace his steps. In yet another sign of his inexperience, he discovered at an old camp a pair of crampons – cleats for ice climbing – that would have been extremely useful but he tossed them away. Finally, after five days and facing worsening weather, he returned down the mountain, snow blind, exhausted and in great pain from a badly twisted ankle.

But 18 days later, on May 12 he again set forth and this time he did take two of the Sherpas with him. With their guidance and knowledge of the terrain, after just three days of climbing the group worked their way to Camp III.

Bad weather kept the group in the camp for several days. Refusing to allow the Sherpas to accompany him any further, on May 21 Wilson began his climb toward the summit, heading to Camp IV. He spent five days making slow progress and having to camp on ledges exposed to the freezing winds. Finally, he encountered an impassable forty foot ice wall blocking his route that sent him back to Camp III where the Sherpas had been waiting.

When urged by the Sherpas to return down the mountain to the monastery, Wilson rebuffed them and insisted on making one final attempt, writing in his diary "this will be a last effort, and I feel successful."[3]

On May 29, he headed back up the mountain, alone. That night he pitched a new camp several hundred yards above the Sherpas' camp, where he remained the following day, in bed resting. On May 31, 1934, after noting in his diary, "Off again, gorgeous day,"[4] he broke camp to make his final climb, determined to find a route to reach the summit of Mt. Everest.

Edmund Hillary and the 1953 British Everest Expedition

Nineteen years after Maurice Wilson took on Everest, the British mounted their ninth Everest expedition. As Britain's Royal Geographical Society describes it:

> In 1953, under the leadership of John Hunt, the British were given permission to climb Mount Everest. Hunt brilliantly orchestrated the necessary equipment and scientific preparations and, through his belief in teamwork, brought together a band of men who together would attempt this lofty peak.[5]

The British expedition consisted of over 400 people, including 362 porters, twenty experienced Sherpa guides from Nepal and over 10,000 pounds of equipment in support of fewer than 20 climbers.

New Zealander Edmund Hillary was among the climbers recruited to join the effort. An experienced mountaineer, Hillary had been a member of a British reconnaissance expedition to Everest in 1951.

Early on, Hunt selected two climbing pairs to attempt to reach the summit. For one of the pairs, Hillary would be partnered with Sherpa Tenzing Norgay. Norgay, one of the most experienced guides with the expedition, had set a new climbing altitude record the previous year, reaching a height less than 1,000 feet from Everest's summit.

Edmund Hillary on
Mt. Everest, 1953

---

3 Maurice Wilson's diary, Alpine Club archives, quoted in Unsworth.
4 *Ibid.*
5 "Mount Everest Expedition 1953." ImagingEverest.rgs.org. Retrieved 07-27-2012.

The expedition's journey started from Base Camp, established in March 1953, with the team following their map, slowly working their way up the mountain to a succession of advanced camps. After about two months, on May 21, they set up final camp at 25,900 ft, about 3,000 feet from the summit.

On May 28, after the first climbing pair came within 300 vertical feet but failed to reach the peak, Hunt sent Hillary and the Sherpa Norgay, with a three-man support team, to make a final assault on Everest's summit. Two days later, Hillary led Tenzing on a terrifying maneuver up a sheer 40-foot rock face. Past this obstacle, the two found a relatively simple climb to the peak. In Hillary's words, "A few more whacks of the ice axe in the firm snow, and we stood on top."[6] At 11:30 am on May 29, 1953, Edmund Hillary became the first person to reach the highest spot on earth, the summit of Mt. Everest.

A moment later Tenzing stepped to the summit. After Hillary took a few pictures, Tenzing buried some chocolates in the snow as an offering and Hillary buried a small cross that had been a gift from John Hunt. That done, the two men began their slow descent down Everest.

Once thought to be insurmountable, Mt. Everest finally had been conquered by a committed team supported by expert guides, the right tools and a good map.

Postscript

In 1935, a small British Everest reconnaissance expedition discovered Maurice Wilson's body just below Camp IV, far from the summit, lying in a snowdrift and wrapped in the shredded remains of his tent. The climbers buried his body in a nearby crevasse. Like the chocolates and cross left by Norgay and Hillary, Wilson's body remains on Everest to this day, a morbid memorial to his lonely, ill-prepared and ill-fated journey.

Today, almost 25 years after his death, Sir Edmund Hillary remains a legend and an internationally known figure. Maurice Wilson, meanwhile, is unknown to the world at large, a mere footnote in the history of Mt. Everest; he's known only to a few in the mountaineering community as that eccentric Brit who foolishly tried to climb Mt. Everest on his own.

---

[6] PBS, NOVA, "First to Summit." Retrieved 07-28-2012.

If you don't have a plan for yourself,
you'll be part of someone else's.
   —American Proverb

A road well begun is the battle half
won. The important thing is to make a
beginning and get under way.
   —Soren Kierkegaard

Introduction

WARNING: If you haven't read the Everest stories in the Prologue, little of the following will make sense to you. Go back and read it. It's interesting.

For those adventurers like Maurice Wilson and Edmund Hillary who seek Everest's summit, it really is a do-or-die proposition. Hunkering down will result in frostbite, hypothermia and death. Success requires that you continue moving forward, climbing toward your goal. Of course, you can give up and return to base camp, although it's a fact that more climbers die descending than ascending the mountain.

Of course, this book isn't about mountain climbing. It's about employee benefits agencies, their future in the post-healthcare reform world, and how the benefits agency can be reinvented to thrive in this new world.

The stories in the Prologue, however, have tremendous implications for the agency leader who is serious about reinventing his agency. More about that later.

Do or Die. The title makes it sound like this book is about serious business. And it is.

For most benefits agencies, how the leadership responds to the recent and impending changes in our industry are a matter of life and death for the agency. For the vast majority of benefits agencies, the status quo business model is no longer sufficient for success...or even survival. For the agency, it *is* do or die.

Along with almost every other industry expert, I'm predicting a major shake out for benefits agencies, with consolidations, acquisitions and closures expected to greatly thin the herd. The few winners in each market will be the agencies that can transform themselves to adapt to the new realities...and new opportunities.

Dramatic agency attrition

MarshBerry, one of the industry's leading mergers & acquisitions consulting firms, have stated that the benefits agency with annual revenue below $2.5 million will struggle to survive. They project that over the next five to eight years the number of benefits agencies with revenue less than $2.5 million will *decrease 28.6 percent* while the number of agencies generating above $2.5 million will increase 26.3 percent.[7]

28.6 percent...that's approaching one in three smaller agencies that will cease to exist, either from closure or acquisition, over the next several years. And I suspect that's too conservative. MarshBerry may be assuming that more agency leaders actually will change their business model to adapt to the new circumstances than is likely the case.

So what should an agency leader do who wants to remain in business, wants to remain relevant and profitable? That's exactly the question that this book answers.

I want to make two critical points here:

1)   While I've written this book for the principals and leaders of U.S. employee benefits agencies, even if you're an agency leader, this book may not be for you. The intended audience for this book is a small subset of agency leaders.

2)   This book is not for thinking, it's for *doing.*

Let me address point one first: **So, is this book for you?**

If you've got that "deer in the headlight" look on your face and you're frozen in place, unable to decide what, if anything, you can do, this book is not for you....unless you're willing to shake it off and act now.

If you're looking frantically for the exits and praying for a white knight to acquire your agency or at least your block of business, this book is not for you.

If you are sitting tight, refusing to change, and praying for the Republicans to repeal Obamacare and restore the status quo from 2009, this book is not for you.

(Even with full repeal, the genie isn't going back in the bottle. The carriers have announced that the changes effected by PPACA since 2010 – including changes in compensation – are here to stay. It's a brand new industry, either way.)

---

7 *Leader's Edge Magazine M&A Review 2011.* LeadersEdgeMagazine.com. Retrieved 08-11-2012.

If your plan is to keep on doing what you've been doing in the past, this book *certainly* isn't for you. (Good luck with that strategy, by the way.)

But...

If you look at our industry today and see – not an industry at risk – but exciting new opportunities forming from the crisis created by PPACA, *this book is for you.*

If you sense an opportunity to gain huge market share in the next several years, *this book is for you.*

If you are ready – even eager – to embrace the changes needed for your agency to both survive PPACA and capitalize on the unparalleled new opportunities, *this book most definitely is for you.*

Team, guides, tools, map

If you are ready to adopt the necessary changes and new business model in your agency to seize the coming opportunities, then you should be wondering, "What exactly should I do... and how should I do it?"

The obvious lesson to draw from the stories of Edmund Hillary and Maurice Wilson in the Prologue is the difficulty of climbing to the top of Mt. Everest without peer support and expert guidance and without the proper tools and map.

Wilson was brave and fiercely committed, to be sure but also quite delusional. He never fully appreciated the terrific challenge he was facing.

Edmund Hillary and the British Everest Expedition suffered no delusions whatsoever. They fully recognized the fierce nature of the challenge and mounted a well-funded effort complete with a committed team, expert guides, all the right tools, and a good map to give them every advantage in conquering the summit.

You're not wanting to climb to the top of Everest, I realize. You are, however – I have to assume – committed to surviving the coming shakeout and, in the process, climbing to the top of our industry in your market.

While your journey of reinvention isn't quite a climb to the top of Everest, it is a daunting task, nonetheless.

Your climb to the top

My friend and fellow Contributing Editor at *Employee Benefit Adviser* magazine, Jack Kwicien – agency consultant and mergers & acquisitions expert – recently advised agency leaders – quite correctly – that "you likely have to change your *marketing, sales* and *client engagement approach*, as well as your *business model*."[8] (emphasis added) Such comprehensive change will not be easy; your success will require deliberate and intensive effort.

You won't succeed simply by trying to graft a couple of new strategies on-to your agency. To reinvent your agency you must make a full commitment to change and adopt an in-depth plan for agency transformation that you can have in place quickly.

You can guess that I am a firm believer in the teamwork approach and taking advantage of peer support, expert guides, the right tools and the right map.

But at the very least, you need a good map.

Your map for the climb

This book is your detailed map for transforming your agency to become reform proof and capable of dominating your market in the post-reform world. This is a practical, step-by-step, how-to guide for you to reinvent your agency with a new business model known as the 21st Century Agency.

So, here's a million dollar – or fill in your agency's annual revenue – question for you:

What does the post-reform 21st Century Agency look like?

The benefits agency business model that worked for you yesterday... simply won't work tomorrow. Much of it no longer works today.

Those who stick with the old-school business model will either sell their book or be acquired, if they're lucky. Many will have to shut their doors and walk away empty handed.

As more agency leaders across the country have begun to recognize this reality, many have been asking me what they must do to remain relevant and profitable.

The 21st Century Agency

The book you are holding in your hands contains not only my answer to their question but a comprehensive map for agency reinvention as a 21st Century Agency.

For several years, my co-author and business partner, Scott Cantrell, and I have been consulting with agencies across the country – large and small – to help them improve their sales and marketing for greater top-line revenue and to streamline their operations for efficiency and more bottom-line income.

---

[8] "The Path to Consultancy." *Employee Benefit Adviser.* August 2012.

This book's plan for transforming your business into a 21st Century Agency includes the foundational elements of the consultative selling system, high-ROI marketing strategies, and the agency and sales management techniques and strategies that we provide our private consulting clients.

Four steps to reinvention

The 21st Century Agency plan is broken down into four easy-to-understand steps that address the key areas of transformation your agency must undergo.

In our work with agencies, we've identified four critical areas for agency transformation necessary for an agency to survive the next five years and emerge a long-term winner:

> ➤ **Portfolio**

> ➤ **Marketing & prospecting**

> ➤ **Selling style**

> ➤ **Agency & sales management**

This book lays out in simple terms what you must do to transform your agency in those specific areas. It shows you what and how you need to implement these changes in your business.

Reaching the summit

This map will get you from Point A to Point B.

Point A is where your agency is today, your Base Camp, if you will, at the foot of the mountain. Point B is where you want to be, as soon as possible, the top of the mountain, that point where your business is now a 21st Century Agency, reform proof and ready to challenge for dominance in your market.

It won't be easy

I'm not suggesting this will be easy. It won't. It won't be easy for you or your team.

If it were easy, every agency would do it. Winning isn't easy; if it were, losers would do it.

These four areas for reinvention encompass almost everything you do as an agency. And that's my point. This is a big deal. Not impossible. But it's a lot to do. And it's a lot to do by yourself.

Your choice, however, is do it...or die as an agency.

Again, this book shows you what exactly to do and how to do it.

If you're thinking right now that you would like some help reinventing your agency, in Chapter 21 I'll show you how to get some serious help to make agency reinvention happen in your business much more easily and quickly.

Take action

Remember my second point above, that this book is not for thinking, it's for doing?

Ideas are cheap but action is priceless. These ideas are powerful. And they're *worthless* unless you take them and do.

Like the title says, it's DO or die.

Selling is about helping your prospects make decisions that solve their problems, so I urge you to influence your own decision-making process. You almost never have all the information you need to make risk-free decisions. But you can use the map and the proven strategies in this book to guide your steps.

Because you are reading this book, I doubt you are the type to let the decision you put off today to reform-proof your agency become the regrets that haunt you in the future.

The management guru Peter Drucker wrote, "Wherever you see a successful business, someone once made a courageous decision."

Both Maurice Wilson and Edmund Hillary made the courageous decision to climb to the summit of Everest. Only one made it and got to enjoy his success and talk about it later.

On returning to base camp from Everest's summit, Hillary's first words to his fellow climber and lifelong friend George Lowe were, "Well, George, we knocked the bastard off."

If you diligently will follow the plan laid out in this book, in 12 months or however long your journey, you will have a 21st Century Agency.

When you've reached the summit, I want you to contact me and announce, "Well, Nelson, we knocked the bastard off."

You now have the map to the summit. Good luck!

Section ONE

Danger, Chaos & Opportunity

When written in Chinese, the word
"crisis" is composed of two characters.

One represents "danger," and the
other represents "opportunity."
 —John F. Kennedy

WEI-CHI (CRISIS)

For the first time in history, the ground is shifting beneath employee benefits agencies, causing a massive crisis in our industry.

Déjà vu all over again

There's no question that it seems like we've been here before. Veteran brokers are experiencing déjà vu all over again. Over the past forty years, brokers have seen numerous major federal legislation and regulations affecting our industry:

1974...ERISA.

1978...Section 125.

1985...COBRA.

1996...HIPAA.

With every major new federal regulatory regime up until now, the industry has first cried, "The sky is falling" and then fairly easily adapted to the new realities.

From ERISA through HIPAA, the benefits industry – carriers and agencies alike – absorbed the changes, even found opportunity in them, and life continued much as it had since the 1960s.

Until 2010...PPACA.

Richter magnitude 9.2

There is, however, an important difference between PPACA and what's come before. The major regulatory changes before PPACA were largely superficial and did not affect the underlying structure of the benefits industry. While brokers had to learn to work with and accommodate new regulatory and compliance requirements, the foundations of the carrier/broker and broker/client relationships remained largely untouched. Broker compensation, plan design, funding, and the broker role were mostly unaffected.

Today, however, the sky still isn't falling but the ground is shaking. Obamacare is effectively a massive earthquake that has demolished the industry's foundations and represents the most wrenching structural upheaval ever seen in our industry. Put in geological terms, PPACA would be the equivalent of an earthquake registering, let's say, 9.2 on the Richter scale, the same magnitude of the 2004 Indian Ocean earthquake, triggering what is now known as the South Asian tsunami. According to Wikipedia:

The earthquake... triggered a series of devastating tsunamis along the coasts of the Indian Ocean, killing over 230,000 people in fourteen countries, and inundating coastal communities with waves up to 98 ft. high. It was one of the deadliest natural disasters in recorded history.[9]

PPACA's regulatory tsunami which makes land on Wednesday, January 1st, 2014, will inundate the benefits landscape and drown every benefits agency that doesn't seek higher ground.

With the full tsunami hitting soon, does this mean the industry is doomed? Should benefits brokers be looking for a new job selling life insurance or maybe a sales rep position with one of the employee benefits technology firms? No, of course not. Our industry is capable of more resiliency and innovation than that.

Does it mean that brokers and agencies must do some changing themselves? Yes, I guarantee it.

After all, I entitled this book *DO OR DIE*. The "do" is all about changing your business model and how you do business so that you can survive the current crisis and capitalize on the opportunities that the crisis is creating.

Opportunity in the crisis

As you read at the beginning of this section, the Chinese character for "crisis" includes the characters for both "danger" and "opportunity." Rightly so.

With PPACA and the crisis in our industry, the danger for benefits agencies is obvious. Change or expect to be acquired or out of business within five years. Do or die.

The opportunities are not as obvious but they are certainly there. In this book, you'll discover some of the main opportunities that we see for your agency. And I'll reveal just how to reposition your agency to take advantage of these opportunities.

Crisis... chaos... change... they always create opportunity. PPACA is changing the rules and changing incentives. The earthquake is blocking old revenue streams but opening up new revenue opportunities for the smart brokers and agency leaders.

Both despite and because of Obamacare, employers are facing more challenges than ever around their employee benefits, including:

---

9 "2004 Indian Ocean earthquake and tsunami." www.Wikipedia.com. Retrieved 06-07-2012.

> ➢ Continued medical inflation;

> ➢ Increased compliance requirements;

> ➢ New benefits funding options;

> ➢ Employee health management;

> ➢ Meeting benefits needs of four generations;

> ➢ Employee retention & recruitment;

> ➢ Benefits communication; and

> ➢ Benefits technology options.

Employers need for their brokers to provide guidance, expertise and help with a wide range of problems for which the employer doesn't have solutions and opportunities that the employer simply doesn't recognize. Yet few agencies are prepared to go beyond spreadsheeting the medical and jiggering the plan design. These agencies occupy the lowest ground in the industry and are the most at risk from the coming flood waters of PPACA. They have no future unless they are willing to change.

New opportunity

That blinding light that has brokers frozen in their tracks isn't the benefits industry imploding. It's the flash of creation as a huge new opportunity is forming...for the wise ones willing to both see and seize it.

An unprecedented opportunity is emerging for keen-eyed, nimble brokers who will reposition their agency for post-reform success.

Are you game? Are you ready to dominate your market?

The market is changing, true. But your competitors are frozen, standing flat-footed, mouths agape, eyes wide with fear. Are you ready to outmaneuver them, to take action and own the future?

The future belongs to the benefits agency that will climb the mountain and move beyond the spreadsheeting and quote-carrying of the past to the higher ground of providing consultative services, wellness and population health management services, innovative technology solutions to HR problems, superior communications, and value-added services. This is the opportunity.

But many agency leaders can't get past their focus on the change agent, PPACA, to see this opportunity. In this first section of the book, I lay out the case for ignoring Obamacare – why it shouldn't matter for your and your agency, not once you move your agency up the mountain to provide clients higher-level services. I discuss why so many agency leaders and brokers can't see the opportunity and what will open their eyes to the remarkable opportunity they have to dominate their market.

And since you know where you are – where your Point A is – I walk you through the benefits agency of the future, the 21st Century Agency, to give you a sense of where you're going – your Point B at the summit of the mountain.

Finally, I'll give you the four steps to becoming a 21st Century Agency, the framework for the rest of the book and your map for reaching the summit and leaving the devastation from PPACA far behind you.

[W]hy make a fuss over something that's done anyway? I was never one to obsess about the past. Too much to do in the future!
 —Edmund Hillary

1

The Clock Is Ticking…
And Why It Just
Doesn't Matter

I n this classic movie still, legendary
silent film comedian Harold Lloyd hangs
from the minute hand of a large clock
high above the street. This iconic image
came to me while thinking of a benefits
broker desperately trying to stop the steady,
ominous ticking of the clock toward
Wednesday, January 1st, 2014 – when the
full implementation of Obamacare is slated
to come crashing down on benefits agencies
and the industry. With the decision by the
Supreme Court to uphold PPACA and the
November 2012 election results, the clock
is most surely ticking....

BUT IT DOESN'T MATTER.

Let me repeat that. It just doesn't matter.

Because Obamacare just doesn't matter. Not for your benefits business.

PPACA is a huge disaster for American healthcare and our liberties, yes. But, for your benefits business, Obamacare just doesn't matter. That is, not if you will choose to reinvent your agency to both adapt to the new realities and capitalize on the new opportunities.

Still not fully aware of the magnitude of the coming tsunami, most benefits agencies continue in their old ways, even though brokers have had to roll up their pants legs as the initial flood waters of PPACA rise above their ankles.

The coming flood

But the roar of the coming tsunami tells the tale....

The very future of small group health insurance is in question. You've heard the evidence. Lockton Benefit Group has predicted that almost 20 percent of employers may drop their employee health care coverage.[10] McKinsey & Company projects that 30 percent of firms likely will eliminate their employer-sponsored insurance once the state exchanges are in place.[11] While opinions vary wildly on the actual impact that guaranteed issue and the exchanges will have on employer-sponsored small group insurance, there is no question that in 2014 PPACA will change the rules, the incentives and the options facing employers. There's also no question that some percentage of employers (my guess: 35-40 percent within three years) will drop their small group coverage.

Agencies stand to lose a large percentage of their book... *unless they change their strategy and business model.*

Agency compensation is also in question...and under fire. Again, no surprise to you unless you've been living in solitary confinement. PPACA's Medical Loss Ratios first led medical carriers to reduce commissions, savagely for individual health plans, less so for group medical plans. But the changes are continuing. There is a trend in small group of carriers moving to a per-employee commission, delinking commissions from premiums and ending the upward commission creep due to medical inflation.

---

[10] "Employer Health Reform Survey Results" (June 2011). Health Reform Advisory Practice. Lockton Companies, Inc., p. 8.

[11] Singhal, Shubham; Jeris Stueland, and Drew Ungerman. "How US Health Care Reform Will Affect Employee Benefits" (June 2011). McKinsey Quarterly, p. 2.

Now, in an even more troubling trend, leading medical carriers are moving to eliminate commissions entirely for large group plans (over 50 or 100 lives, depending on the carrier), forcing brokers into a fee-for-service model. While not all carriers have yet imposed this new compensation model nationwide, there's no doubt this is the future for large group medical.

Benefits agencies stand to lose a major percentage of their revenues... *unless they change their strategy and business model.*

So the industry is changing in structural ways and benefits agencies have begun to feel the impact. And PPACA hasn't even been implemented yet.

But those agency leaders that recognize the imperative for change and are prepared to adopt a new business model can avoid the ravages of PPACA that many agencies will experience as their businesses crumble.

This book provides the motivated and visionary agency principal with a new business model we call the 21st Century Agency. For over 60 years, most benefits agencies have operated on a business model that developed in the mid-20th century following the creation of employer-sponsored insurance. That old business model has changed little over the decades. Even though we are well into the 21st century, few agencies moved beyond the 20th century agency model. I admit there has been little incentive for agency principals to make the effort.

Now would be the time

A couple of years ago, while driving in downtown Nashville during a heavy rainstorm, my partner, Scott, and I saw a man walking on the sidewalk with a large umbrella.

But even with the rain coming down hard, he was holding his umbrella by his side, closed. "Now would be the time," Scott commented wryly, as we watched in dismay as the downpour soaked the man while he held his furled umbrella useless at his side.

You have to wonder about the guy, walking in the midst of a rainstorm, carrying an umbrella but never using it.

There may have been little incentive in the past for an agency to adopt a modern business model but with PPACA about to wreak havoc on our industry and make the old business model totally obsolete, now would be the time. The 21st Century Agency is designed to make your agency reform proof, impervious to PPACA's devastation.

Transforming into a 21st Century Agency will require changes to your agency's portfolio, marketing, selling and management. Yes, that's a lot of change but the changes actually are quite organic and symbiotic, once you begin to implement the new business model.

The difference between the old-school agency business model and the new-school 21st Century Agency model is the emphasis on increased value... more value for the client and more value for the agency principal.

High ROI

The 21st Century Agency is characterized by *high ROI* (return on investment), seen in greater value for the client and strict accountability from the agency's marketing, sales and operations. The client gets a greater return on its broker investment and the agency demands a higher return on its investment in back office, marketing and producers.

Giving the client greater value provides your agency with a competitive advantage, increases retention, and, perhaps most important, positions your agency for the inevitable move to a fee-based model.

Holding your marketing, back office and producers truly accountable increases productivity and drives more revenue to your bottom line. With lower profit margins, there is no margin for error in operations or sales. Lean and efficient is the only model that will survive.

The competition clock

ObamaCare just doesn't matter.

Not if you are willing to see the new opportunity, embrace the 21st Century Agency business model, and move quickly to implement it.

Come 2014, whether ObamaCare is implemented or repealed, for the 21st Century Agency it just won't matter. You'll own your market either way.

The ticking clock that matters isn't Obamacare's countdown to 2014. The sound you should be paying full attention to is the sound of the competition clock ticking away....

The race isn't against the implementation of Obamacare, it's the race with your competitors to be first to market with the game-changing strategies and business model that will allow you to capitalize on the new opportunities and dominate your market.

Each problem has hidden in it an opportunity so powerful that it literally dwarfs the problem. The greatest success stories were created by people who recognized a problem and turned it into an opportunity.

—Joseph Sugarman

A pessimist is one who makes difficulties of his opportunities and an optimist is one who makes opportunities of his difficulties.

—Harry Truman

2

Opportunity Is Knocking...
Do You Hear It?

For a few readers, this chapter may be unnecessary but for most it will be essential in providing you with the ability to move past personal feelings about the new world in which we now live. Only by taking this vital first step and recognizing that our challenging situation is, in fact, a historic opportunity, will any agency leader be able to move forward productively and profitably.

A brief history of this opportunity...it's not that new, really

Even before the 2008 elections, my team and I at Bottom Line Solutions began planning for significant healthcare reform. While the writing wasn't officially on the wall, the Democrats were already getting out their graffiti spray cans.

I'd been down this road before, in 1992 during my days in public policy running a couple of think tanks. I was a veteran of the fight against Hillarycare, the Clinton administration's attempt at healthcare reform. We won that battle but I feared that the Obama healthcare reform effort couldn't be stopped. I was right.

Initially, just like many benefits brokers and agencies today, we were very concerned for the viability and future of the industry. However, after applying some creative problem-solving and carefully examining the most likely outcomes, we realized there would be a tremendous opportunity for those agencies that did not give up after fighting a losing battle but instead decided to transform their business. We envisioned a transformation – or reinvention – that not only would give these reinvented agencies the ability to survive reform but also have the capacity to grow and dominate their markets.

Thus, at the beginning of 2009, when the healthcare reform debate began to heat up, our firm began promoting the remarkable opportunity that would be available to those agencies that would recognize it and embrace it.

During that time, much of the industry was in denial, not really believing that reform would ever become a reality. And while we were hopeful that the Obama effort would fail, we also considered the very real probability of health reform and created a simple plan to transform benefits agencies into businesses that could withstand any likely reform and flourish in the face of whatever regulatory changes occurred.

In other words, my team and I developed a plan that would take the sting out of reform. The best part was, as I described in the last chapter, for agencies that adopted this straightforward strategic plan, reform simply wouldn't matter.

All that to say, that simple little plan from over four years ago has now become greatly expanded and much more refined and specific. This now comprehensive plan is detailed in the pages of this book. And the strategies laid out here will work regardless of what health reform eventually looks like. Ironically, this plan should have been implemented by benefits agencies long ago, as it provides for steady, sustained growth as well as strengthens longterm client relationships and increases the value of each client, creating a higher overall valuation of the business.

Regardless, adopting this plan for agency reinvention is no longer an option for an agency leader who wants to survive and thrive post reform. With SCOTUS upholding the constitutionality of PPACA, with key sections of the law already in effect (e.g., the Medical Loss Ratio requirements), and with the medical carriers promising to retain the elements already enacted, our industry has changed. And it's not changing back. Simply put, the die has been cast.

The first step...recognizing the opportunity

To take advantage of the massive opportunity presented by reform, you must accept the fact that the healthcare industry has been, is being, and will continue to be reformed. (Reform had to occur. The status quo before PPACA was entirely unsustainable, providing almost no incentives for health, wellness and prevention, and perverse incentives for health providers.) In order to succeed despite these reforms, you must move past any personal anger and disappointment. As Edmund Hillary stated, "[W]hy make a fuss over something that's done anyway?" If you cannot or will not let go of those negative attitudes, you can never expect to be excited or motivated about the opportunity that is now yours for the taking.

Just as much as anger, resentment, and disappointment will virtually guarantee failure, so will ignorance, uncertainty and straight-up fear.

Head in the sand

So many otherwise smart, savvy leaders in our industry are suffering from what I call The Ostrich Syndrome.

You can guess...but it looks something like this...

Burying your head in the sand (literally or figuratively) and pretending like the issue doesn't exist will not make it go away. In fact, choosing ignorance, assuming that everything will work out, and doing nothing is the worst possible action for principals in the post-reform world.

At least those who choose not to adopt the plan laid out in this book and instead consciously choose to close up shop or sell off their agency or their book of business have made a choice based on the reality of the challenge. For most principals the decision simply to "cash-out" is, in our estimation, a short-sighted and impulsive decision but at least they choose that path and are acknowledging the need for a change. They merely don't have the vision or the will to take advantage of the massive opportunity before them.

So if you ever find yourself "doing business as usual" when you know real change is required, pull your head up out of the sand, look around, and make a proactive, intentional decision – ideally one that seizes the opportunity and leaves you much better off than you were previously.

Jim Rohn on Opportunity

I never miss a chance to share the insights of Jim Rohn:

An enterprising person is one who comes across a pile of scrap metal and sees the making of a wonderful sculpture. An enterprising person is one who drives through an old decrepit part of town and sees a new housing development. An enterprising person is one who sees opportunity in all areas of life.

To be enterprising is to keep your eyes open and your mind active. It's to be skilled enough, confident enough, creative enough and disciplined enough to seize opportunities that present themselves... regardless of the economy.

To be enterprising is to keep your eyes open and your mind active. It's to be skilled enough, confident enough, creative enough and disciplined enough to seize opportunities that present themselves... regardless of the economy.

A person with an enterprising attitude says, "Find out what you can before action is taken." Do your homework. Do the research. Be prepared. Be resourceful. Do all you can in preparation of what's to come.

Enterprising people always see the future in the present. Enterprising people always find a way to take advantage of a situation, not be burdened by it. And enterprising people aren't lazy. They don't wait for opportunities to come to them, they go after the opportunities. Enterprise means always finding a way to keep yourself actively working toward your ambition.

Enterprise is two things. The first is creativity. You need creativity to see what's out there and to shape it to your advantage. You need creativity to look at the world a little differently. You need creativity to take a different approach, to be different.

What goes hand-in-hand with the creativity of enterprise is the second requirement: the courage to be creative. You need courage to see things differently, courage to go against the crowd, courage to take a different approach, courage to stand alone if you have to, courage to choose activity over inactivity.

And lastly, being enterprising doesn't just relate to the ability to make money. Being enterprising also means feeling good enough about yourself, having ugh self worth to want to seek advantages and opportunities that will make a difference in your future. And by doing so you will increase your confidence, your courage, your creativity and your self-worth, your enterprising nature.

The critical question

To the critical question at hand, do you believe and truly recognize that there is a significant new opportunity available to you as a benefits broker created by the fear, uncertainty, and fallout from healthcare reform?

I trust you answered in the affirmative.

If you're still unsure as to the viability of the opportunity, I understand. It's appropriate and natural to have serious reservations about reinventing any business, especially one as seemingly complicated and set in its ways as a benefits agency. So, if you're still skeptical as to whether there is any real opportunity or if you think the concept is simply the idealistic ramblings of some overly ambitious and presumptuous so-called "thought leader," here's my recommendation...keep reading. You owe it to yourself and, just as critically, you owe it to your business.

As you go through the following pages and more specifics are delivered to you chapter after chapter, I suspect you'll quickly realize just how real and achievable this goal of "reinventing your business into a 21st Century Agency" really is, and thus, how you can take advantage of this truly limited-time opportunity centered around reform.

Two quick disclaimers

DISCLAIMER #1 The plan in this book represents nothing new under the sun. In fact, each primary concept, strategy and even the specific tactics have been employed successfully as best practices in other industries and, in many cases already are being used by some progressive agencies that recognized the benefit of reinvention prior to it becoming a necessity thanks to Obamacare.

DISCLAIMER #2 This opportunity to reinvent your agency, keep it relevant, viable and ultimately achieve higher levels of success than you have currently will not be completed overnight. Nor will it be easy. It will take some dogged determination and commitment to see it through to fruition. In the words of Thomas Edison, someone who knows something about opportunity – not to mention reinvention and determination – "Opportunity is missed by most people because it is dressed in overalls and looks like work."

Yes, it will take some work but the way I see it, you'll be working anyway so why not make that work as productive and profitable as possible?!

Finally, let me leave you with a statement and an image that I've been using in nearly every presentation I've given to benefits brokers over the past four years....

When Opportunity Knocks...

You Never Know WHAT It Will Look Like!

You'll never leave where
you are, until you decide
where you'd rather be.
  —Robert Brockman

3

Touring A
21ˢᵗ Century Agency

To reposition your agency for post reform success, you have to embark on a journey of reinvention. You know the current state of your agency, which we'll call Point A, the 20ᵗʰ century business model. This book will give you a detailed map to guide you on a journey to move your agency from Point A to a Point B where your business is now a 21ˢᵗ Century Agency. So just what does that new business model look like? Let's take a guided tour of a typical 21ˢᵗ Century Agency.

As you walk in the front door of the 21ˢᵗ Century Agency you are visiting, you initially notice nothing different than you would expect to see in a thriving employee benefits agency.

In-bound prospect calls from marketing

Everything seems normal, until you notice that the receptionist is finding it difficult to do more than acknowledge you with a nod and a smile because of the continuous inbound phone calls she has to answer before transferring the caller. The agency's new marketing campaign is generating a large volume of calls from prospect company HR departments requesting more information or a meeting with one of the agency's EB advisors.

Finally, during a temporary lull, she is able to say hello and get your name and the person you are there to see. After a quick call by the receptionist, you're greeted by the administrative assistant who informs you the president is still in his daily morning sales meetings with producers and offers to take you on a quick tour of the agency. Accepting the offer, you follow her back into the administrative area.

Automated direct mail

As you pass one cubicle, your guide tells you that the customer service rep (CSR) sitting there has just spent a total of 15 minutes online to send a direct mail greeting card to every client as one of this month's communication contacts. The card features a whimsical St. Patrick's Day theme and a message in the president's handwriting, will have a handwritten address and an actual stamp, yet the agency staff will never see the cards, touch the cards, hand-write a single word, address or stamp a single envelope. Leveraging the power of technology, the agency uses an automated system for the entire direct mail process and pays just $1.43 per greeting card...including postage. The agency is able to build a relationship with its clients while keeping costs low and not tying up staff on tedious and low-value tasks.

Done-for-you client newsletters

The CSR next will go to another website to confirm that the agency's two print newsletters have been sent, one to their HR clients, the other for the *employees* of their client companies. They began sending a newsletter to market directly to employees once the agency expanded its portfolio to include workplace home & auto and voluntary benefits, Medicare supplement plans, retirement plans, and individual long-term care policies. Both the HR and the employee newsletters are turnkey done-for-you products that the agency staff doesn't have to produce and never even see until the agency's copies of the HR newsletter comes in the mail and the employee newsletters arrive in bulk to be delivered personally to the client's offices by producers.

Outsourced appointment setter

Your attention is directed to another office staff member who is on a brief call with the outsourced appointment setter. Paid $10 per hour, she makes prospecting calls to targeted business prospects offering a complimentary PPACA compliance review and sets appointments for producer meetings. This valuable but low-level task used to be done by a CSR, who is now free for more important tasks.

Outsourced social media marketing

In a moment, that same staffer will end her call and will make another call to the outsourced social media marketing manager who maintains and updates the agency's social media presence on its blog, Facebook, LinkedIn and Twitter for just $250 per month. The owner and the producers provide him the content, you're informed, and he updates all the platforms, ensuring regular updates and Tweets, saving the office staff multiple hours a week, and freeing them for more high value tasks.

Automated email and prospecting lead magnet

Then this staffer will turn her attention to the agency's email auto-responder system that automatically responds to prospect requests by sending a PDF of one of the agency's lead magnets, a special report, "Bend Your Employee Health Trend Curve & Cut Your Benefits Costs By 15%." After a follow-up call from a producer to the prospect, the auto-responder will drip on the prospect for eight weeks with a weekly benefits management tip.

Agency automation system and SOP

Your guide tells you that, before your arrival, she had been working on the agency automation system that serves as the agency's central nervous system. She had been monitoring the CSR client service activity over the past month, tracking the average time required to resolve a client issue and reviewing the results from the automated email client satisfaction survey sent afterward. Later today, she will be updating the agency's Standard Operating Procedures (SOP) manual, which covers every regular customer service, operations, marketing and sales activity.

Consultative and accountable producers

Moving past the admin offices, you stop at the office of a producer who is on the phone. Looking over his shoulder, you notice he's entering his notes from the prospect call he's on into the agency's customer relationship management (CRM) system, a part of the agency automation system. Surprised that a salesman is doing very little of the talking, you hear him asking the prospect a series of probing questions about her goals and challenges, generating answers that go into the CRM. Glancing down at his desk, you notice a weekly calendar scheduled with daily prospecting activities.

Producer rainmaking and health trend assessment

Moving down the hall to another producer's office, you see a young woman rehearsing the presentation she's giving to the Rotary Club later this morning. You learn that, despite her youth, she is one of the top rain makers at the agency; this will be the ninth presentation she's given to civic and business groups in four months. Entitled, "Two Strategies to Reduce Benefits Costs and Boost Your Bottom Line," her talk ends with an offer for a complimentary employee health trend management consultation. The offer has generated nine prospect meetings and two new BOR letters over the past four months.

Principal's high-level activity

Leaving the producer to her rehearsal, you follow your guide down the hall to the president's office just as the third producer departs from the final one-on-one daily sales management meeting. The owner rises to greet you and gestures you to a seat. You notice two large whiteboards on his wall, both filled with rows and columns, one board tracking monthly results from agency marketing activities and the other monthly producer sales numbers.

Diverse portfolio and constant metrics tracking for ROI

The owner notices your interest and mentions that he and his team track all their marketing activity for return on investment (ROI), rolling out the campaigns that do well to a larger list, tweaking marginal performers and retesting, and abandoning the losers. He also points out the sales figures for each producer, broken down by product category, he notes, to track cross-selling success. You comment that you're surprised to see so many product columns. "To begin replacing lost medical commission, we expanded our agency's portfolio with a wide range of products and services," he replies. "Now that we've moved to a fee-for-service model, although our fees average only 65 percent of the commissions we used to get, we're more than making up for it by cross-selling other products and services to solve problems for our clients."

Human resource outsourcing services

His phone rings and, glancing down, he asks your forgiveness while he takes a quick call from the CFO at a 1,500-life account. As he talks, you can't help but overhear him discuss the client's new payroll system that his agency is providing and the work that is underway to integrate that system with the client's benefits administration system from the agency that's already in place. As he ends the call, you hear him laugh in delight at the stellar results of a recent survey on employee satisfaction with the client's benefits plan.

Avatar-guided online self-service enrollment

As he hangs up, he explains to you that there has been a 180 degree turnaround with employee morale at the client company since the agency installed a new online self-service enrollment system for the company's open enrollment. The improvement in employee satisfaction with the benefits, he explains, is due to an avatar-driven benefit communication program built into the enrollment platform that educates the employees on all their benefit options. The avatar is a computer-generated virtual benefit counselor, who can look like anyone or anything and uses a human voice to communicate with employees. "It's highly effective in educating on benefits," he states. "Participation was up in almost every core benefit and 62 percent of employees enrolled in one or more of the new voluntary benefits being offered: Critical Illness, Accident and Universal Life."

Workplace voluntary benefits

"How much do you charge the client for the system?" you ask. "We've knocked the price down to a nominal 10 cents PEPM," he says. "The new voluntary benefits offering paid for giving them the system. Now I've got a very sticky enrollment platform in this key account AND we netted over $100,000 in new commission from the voluntary."

Zealous sales management

Quite impressed, you remember to ask about the morning sales meetings he just finished with each of his producers. "Is this your weekly meeting?" you inquire, curious since it's Tuesday. He informs you that their weekly sales meeting as a team is Monday morning. He meets first thing every morning with each producer individually for five minutes to discuss their planned activities for the day. On Friday afternoon, he meets with each producer one-on-one to review the week's activities. "I can't manage results," he states, "but I can manage activity. And activity is key. The right prospecting and selling activities done consistently produce results."

Managing producers activities yields increased sales results

You ask if he's seen improved sales results, to which he replies, "Since putting this sales management in place, one of my producers has increased his sales by 23 percent, another by 31 percent, and I'm waiting to see about the new one I hired to replace the old one I fired who wouldn't do the activities."

Results-based wellness and employee health trend management

You mention that you heard one of his producers rehearsing a presentation on employee health trend management. He tells you that since the agency started promoting aggressive results-based wellness programs that use financial incentives to move employee health behavior, they have seen dramatic increases in employee participation in the wellness programs and equally dramatic decreases in employee health measurements and plan utilization. "Population health trend management has become not only one of our main ways to drive the client's benefits strategy, it's usually our key to getting in the account in the first place," he says. "It's become one of our primary value propositions."

Greater agency support staff efficiency

In response to your comment about the administrative staff, the president notes that before the agency adopted the 21st Century Agency business model, they had five back office staff. "After we automated and introduced some new systems and we outsourced some lower-value activities, we've been able to reduce our office staff from five to three," he says. "Plus I moved one admin staffer to be my administrative assistant, to whom I now delegate a lot of tasks I used to do personally. You can imagine the boost to our bottom line from all this but the best news is that the agency's – and my personal – operational efficiency and effectiveness have increased substantially. My time has been freed up tremendously."

No more golden handcuffs

After some further discussion about the agency, at 10:30 the president thanks you for your interest and excuses himself. "I've got several items to complete before I head out for lunch with my wife and an afternoon with her at the pool." "On a Tuesday," you say with a smile. "Must be nice."

"Actually, I take three afternoons a week off. he replies. "While I always made good money, in the past I couldn't be away from the office if I wanted things to run right...golden handcuffs, I think they call it. Now, with our new operational and management systems, the agency runs fine without me. Once I hire a sales manager to handle the morning meetings with my producers, I can take off several days each week. Actually, that's in my strategic plan for *next* year."

Back to the 20th century

Thoroughly impressed, you leave and rush back to your agency. In the car, you wonder what your producers are doing and if they have stayed on task without you there. You hope that your entire office staff finally has finished stuffing, labeling and stamping your quarterly client mailing. And you think about all the tedious and low-level tasks on your two-page TO DO List. Then you ask yourself why you're still running a 20th century agency.

The 21st century awaits

You have just seen your future if you reinvent your business as a 21st Century Agency. After you read through this book and implement its plan for agency transformation, these will be just some of the capabilities available to you. I hope you're even more motivated and excited about bringing your business model into this century. Let's get started.

Great things are not done by impulse but by a series of small things brought together.
—George Eliot

Four Steps to Become
A 21ˢᵗ Century Agency

No one doubts that adopting a totally new business model in the face of health-care reform is a massive undertaking, one that we liken to the strenuous and challenging task of climbing Everest to reach the summit.

But, to paraphrase Lao-tzu, a climb of 29,000 feet begins with a single step.

Reinventing your benefits agency into a 21ˢᵗ Century Agency is not a small task. It will require an investment of money, manpower and yes, probably some late nights but ultimately, you simply have to get it done, one step a time.

By now, you should be asking just what are these four steps referenced previously that somehow will allow a benefits agency to not only survive reform but thrive in spite of it? Let's take a look at them now...

The Four Steps of Agency Reinvention

STEP 1 Expand Your Products & Services Portfolio

STEP 2 Reposition Your Agency with High-ROI Marketing

STEP 3 Adopt an Advisory Selling Approach

STEP 4 Manage for Maximum Results

"Oh, is that all?!" you ask.

To survive the thinning of the herd and be a winner in the post-reform world, a benefits agency must reinvent, modify or change just about everything in its business model. A daunting climb? Yes. Do not attempt to make these changes too fast. Simply take them on as we describe in the following pages...one step at a time.

Successful agencies will be those that steadily, day after day, reinvent themselves from the ground up following a proven model. *Out with the old, in with the new business model...the 21st Century Agency.*

The real post-reform winners, those agencies that will acquire the losers and amass market share, will be the agencies that *act* on the imperative for radical and wholesale change.

I know this sounds overwhelming... and possibly demoralizing. And while it is a hard truth, following the same 1-, 2-, 3-, 4-step approach we walk our private and group coaching clients through will provide you a clear, easily followed map for transforming your agency.

Step-by-step

In coming sections of this book, I'll provide you a step-by-step plan that is the foundation of our Agency Growth Mastermind Network program where we walk the members through this entire reinvention process. (See Chapter 21 for more information on this program.) We'll be giving you the critical steps and best practices to transform your agency, make you one of the survivors, make you one of the *winners*.

While each of the steps affects the other three, there is a natural sequence and progression we will use in our discussion of them here and throughout the remainder of the book. This sequence is essentially chronological, although when an agency principal makes the decision to adopt this plan, he most likely will be working on parts of all four steps virtually simultaneously.

While this reinvention will take some concerted work and effort, it is absolutely doable and should not be perceived as impossible. It's merely a process that should must be begun and followed through to its conclusion.

Now let me give you an overview of each of the four steps of agency reinvention that will transform your agency into a 21st Century Agency.

STEP 1 **Expand Your Products & Services Portfolio**

For years, brokers have known the need to cross-sell beyond the traditional core benefits.

Yet most agencies lack a broad portfolio of products and services with which to solve client problems. If you don't have the products and services, you greatly restrict your revenue potential, not to mention restricting your ability to best serve your clients and thus create long-term, valuable relationships.

For a broker to remain viable, relevant and the best choice for his clients, he must have a large toolbox of solutions that he can pull from to eliminate client pain points. Being able to provide meaningful and effective solutions to your clients' problems is a vital ability in the post-reform world.

The days of only offering one or two or three products and expecting to be viewed as a trusted advisor have ended. In the new world of benefits, a broker must become "physician" to his clients – first, diagnosing a client's pain, prescribing a "treatment," and, finally, providing a "cure" in the form of insurance products and valuable services. Only the benefits agency that takes on the role of a true professional advisor, and then supports that role with multiple solutions, an enhanced and full product portfolio, will win and keep their clients.

To their credit, 58 percent of brokers and consultants plan to sell more voluntary benefits, according to MetLife's 2011 Broker and Consultant Study. But voluntary benefits represent only one set of many product and service offerings that you should be making available to your clients.

Building a well-stocked portfolio of both insurance and non-insurance products and services is a necessary step to develop a 21st Century Agency.

STEP 2 Reposition Your Agency with High-ROI Marketing

In our experience with agencies across the U.S., we find that most are extremely inept at marketing their business and prospecting for new clients.

This is completely understandable. Why should insurance agents know how to market and prospect?

I'm being totally serious. Marketing and prospecting isn't taught as part of your insurance school and carriers only offer training on products, so how should an agency leader know effective marketing strategies or be able to teach solid prospecting tactics to his brokers?

Agencies and brokers have done the best they know how in this vital area. But in the post-reform era, an agency that does mediocre, inefficient and costly marketing no longer will be sustainable.

Look, if you're going to offer a larger, more diverse portfolio and provide more solutions and significant value to your clients, you *must* let your prospects know that. So how does a 21st Century Agency differentiate itself from its old-school competition? By spending thousands to put their name and logo on a banner at the golf tournament? Sponsoring a table at the cancer gala? *Please.*

With commissions in decline and a diet of leaner fees on the horizon, agencies can't afford to waste valuable marketing dollars on brand building. All agency spending, especially marketing dollars, must be held accountable. Agencies will need immediate and high return-on-investment (ROI) results from their marketing investment. Likewise, the agency's producers must create serious and meaningful results with their prospecting efforts.

Only through a fresh marketing approach designed to elicit responses from qualified prospects and meaningful conversations with key decision makers will an agency be able to successfully reposition itself and create consistently impressive high-ROI results. This is another essential step to reinventing an agency into a market-dominating 21st Century Agency.

STEP 3 Adopt an Advisory Selling Approach

Most benefits agencies have been transactional, that is, their role has been to facilitate the client's transaction with the carrier to purchase health insurance. Doing a bit of plan design, shopping the carriers, spreadsheeting and then carrying the lowest quote to the client used to earn a substantial commission on the medical...but those days are in the past.

As more than one benefits broker has told me using remarkably similar words, "Brokers have had it far too easy for far too long."

Helping a client get a lower price on a product they already know they must have and intend to buy... that's not selling. And being a human quote engine is no longer sufficient to earn or keep the business.

The days when agency revenues were derived from commissions on the medical and clients had no greater expectation than a low quote are over. Carriers have begun eliminating commissions on large group medical plans, compelling brokers to move to a fee-for-service model.

The majority of brokers and consultants recognize this, according to the MetLife study. Interestingly, the same percentage that plan to sell more voluntary benefits, fifty-eight percent, said they plan to become more consultative in their selling.

To justify the fee to the client, an agency must adopt a consultative approach that provides value by solving client problems and eliminating client pain points. Becoming consultative is one of the key transformations that agencies must effect to become a 21st Century Agency.

STEP 4 Manage for Maximum Results

Much like marketing and prospecting, agency management of operations and sales must become more productive and efficient in the 21st Century Agency. The new economics means there is no margin for error and no place for inefficiency. Agency operations must become leaner and more streamlined, with best practices including internal automation and delegation as well as outsourcing certain tasks to create maximum efficiency.

With lower per-client revenue driving a need for more and better clients, rigorous sales management that demands true accountability is imperative to ensure that producers become more efficient and effective in prospecting and closing sales. As the old saying goes, if you don't measure it, you can't manage it. And if you don't manage it, it's not important. Too many sales organizations are hampered by poor sales management that doesn't really manage producers at all.

Finally, leaders of benefits agencies must know how to properly "keep score" within their business by monitoring key metrics on a consistent basis. Only through quantifying specific activities, successes and failures, will the agency be able to adapt to become even more profitable. It comes down to being able to do more of what works and less of what doesn't work. The only way to achieve the level of power that comes with such knowledge is by tracking, measuring, and applying the critical and quantified information available.

In other words, you have to "keep score." The 21st Century Agency that is able to effectively keep score will have superior sales and operations management and be able to maximize its resources and drive as much top-line revenue as possible to the bottom line.

These four steps represent the framework for any benefits agency to re-invent itself and become a 21st Century Agency capable of not only maintaining its relevance and value post reform but also dominating its market regardless of what happens to PPACA.

Section TWO

21st Century Portfolio
Expanding Your
Agency Toolbox

If you only have a hammer,
you tend to see every problem
as a nail.

  —Abraham Maslow

M any brokers are still using just a hammer in their benefits practice. Too many benefit brokers have been showing up at the jobsite equipped only with the hammer of health insurance, limiting their ability both to add new revenue and to be consultative and solve other HR problems. (Sure, they've got group term life and group long-term disability but these are just commodities already in every employer's benefits plan.)

Without a broad selection of tools – products and services – in the portfolio, brokers never see another problem besides the client's challenges with the health plan. G.K. Chesterton once wrote, "It isn't that they can't see the solution. It's that they can't see the problem." And why should they, if they're not able to offer a solution? Yet the declining revenues from the health insurance hammer demand that brokers create new revenue streams from cross-selling additional products and services. And the growing need to provide greater value to the client by helping solve a range of HR problems demands that brokers have a variety of product and service solutions at hand.

A fully equipped toolbox

To survive the coming industry shakeout, your agency will need a fully stocked toolbox of products and services. Swinging the health insurance hammer – tweaking the plan design and spreadsheeting rates – is no longer sufficient to either get or keep the account.

As the MetLife study cited earlier revealed, almost 60 percent of brokers and consultants report that consultative selling and cross-selling are their two primary strategies for meeting the challenges of the post-reform market. However, a broker can't solve many client problems or cross-sell very much without a broad portfolio of valuable products and services.

A broader portfolio is essential if you want to create new profit centers in your agency.

While products will generate revenue (except, soon, major medical?), services are different. Some services can generate a lucrative fee or a meaningful revenue stream. Other services are value-adds that produce no revenue but can strengthen the broker/client relationship and boost retention. Some services, like benefit strategic planning and benefit administration systems, do both.

Along with a range of products, your agency toolbox must have a strong mix of services that boost your bottom line and/or lock in your client. It's do... or die.

Your 21st Century Agency will boast a loaded toolbox, your hammer joined by a broad range of product and service tools that provide you with valuable solutions, a competitive edge and a healthy bottom line.

CASE STUDY

The Power of a Well-Stocked Toolbox

In the following case study, a D.C.-area broker faces losing the BOR on a lucrative 400-life account because he had just a hammer in his toolbox.

Several years ago, a 400-life construction firm in the D.C.-area was facing a 22-percent renewal on the medical. Looking for relief, HR invited the broker on their construction bonds to quote the medical.

Instead of just spreadsheeting the medical and carrying back the best quote, he took a consultative approach to the account and dug deeper than the client's acknowledged problem with year-over-year increases in their medical premiums. Requesting a meeting with the client, he interviewed the HR director to identify pain points besides the high renewal. He discovered their frustration with the logistics of a paper enrollment, the challenges of communicating benefits to their overwhelmingly Spanish-speaking employees, and the resultant poor participation in the plan. After probing further, however, he discovered that the HR director was under tremendous pressure from the CEO to fix the company's terrible employee retention numbers. The firm's severe turnover problem was due to a competitor that paid an additional dollar per hour, but provided no benefits. Despite a full and generous benefit plan, this company continued to lose employees to the higher hourly rate because HR was unable to communicate the value of their benefit plan to an employee population that spoke only Spanish.

Now understanding the firm's most pressing needs, the broker brought in a new carrier that saved the firm $150,000 on the *current* year's medical premium. Plus, he introduced a benefit communication and enrollment firm that could provide a full Spanish-language enrollment including pre-enrollment communication marketing materials in Spanish and one-on-one meetings for every employee with a bilingual benefit counselor to explain the value of the benefit plan. Finally, he showed how commissions from a new voluntary benefit offering at the workplace would pay for the roughly $17,000 cost of the benefit communication program, meaning zero impact on the company's budget.

Not surprisingly, after learning of the threat to his account, the broker of record *matched his competitor's proposal: the same plan, carrier and cost savings*. But having only a health insurance hammer, he never even recognized the client's turnover problem, more less offered a solution.

The employer awarded the BOR letter to the new broker on the strength of his bilingual enrollment solution to their retention problem. By showing the client how to reduce HR's paperwork and increase plan participation and employee morale with an electronic and bilingual enrollment at no hard-dollar cost, the broker created a proposal that the client couldn't resist and the old broker couldn't match. The benefit communication services and the voluntary benefits in his toolbox gave him the winning edge on the BOR.

Oh, and not only did he earn the medical comp with the BOR, the voluntary benefits offering netted him an additional $43,000 in commission revenue.

Our Age of Anxiety is, in great part, the result of trying to do today's job with yesterday's tools and yesterday's concepts.
  —Marshall McLuhan

5

The New
Toolbox of Solutions

The challenge for the broker seeking to create a 21st Century Portfolio is to identify the right products and services that will allow the agency to:

> Provide a wide range of solutions to client problems;

> Expand and enhance its value proposition; and

> Generate additional revenue streams.

Voluntary benefits and wellness & health trend management are such key additions to your portfolio that they each get their own chapter.

Beyond these two, which in the future will be staples of all successful benefits agencies, you have a large number of valuable and lucrative product and service solutions to choose from. Your choice will depend on your producers and your personal experience and/or preferences. Some of these, such as executive benefits and retirement products and services, which require experience and specialized knowledge to be effective for your client, aren't for every agency. Others, like benefits strategic planning and HR outsourcing services, should be in every agency's toolbox.

While all of these solutions can serve, by definition, a tactical purpose for your clients, they can also serve strategic purposes for your agency, such as helping you reposition yourself in the market or opening up a new industry niche. Another very important strategic purpose would be to help you engage your clients' most important senior executives.

C-Suite in E major

For many brokers and consultants working in the mid-market and up, access to the C-Suite remains the Holy Grail, with the goal of forging a relationship with the executives and becoming a valued strategic partner.

Since the benefit broker's relationship usually is with HR, employee benefits generally does not afford even an introduction to the ultimate decision makers in the executive suite. Viewed by most C-level executives as a mere HR vendor, the vast majority of brokers can only dream of access to the CFO or CEO.

Executive benefits

Offering executive benefits, however, have provided innovative benefit brokers and agencies a direct path into the C-Suite. While executive benefits are certainly a specialized area of our business, to get your agency into the C-Suite you can have one of your brokers trained or you can hire a producer with executive benefits experience. Once in an account, it's just a matter of leveraging the executive relationships to get a shot at the BOR on the benefits. Moreover, not only do executive benefits get you invited into the C-Suite, they are often very remunerative.

Products, however, are just one way to establish a beachhead in the C-Suite. There is one service you definitely should have in your toolbox that will firmly establish you on the client's executive floor.

Benefits strategic planning

Benefits strategic planning is your guaranteed route into the C-Suite.

By its very nature, the benefit strategic planning process must include the CFO and/or CEO, as the architect(s) of the enterprise strategic plan. Since the purpose of benefits strategic planning is to create a sustainable benefits program that aligns with the enterprise strategic plan, the C-level execs must be party to the planning process that the broker will facilitate.

In the mid-market, almost every client will have an enterprise strategic plan. Yet, despite the fact that benefits have become for most companies the largest single operating expense, few have applied the same planning discipline to their benefits plan as they do to the overall enterprise. With benefits strategic planning, the broker works with the company to create an intentional, multi-year planning document that coordinates with the benefits budget requirements of the enterprise strategic plan.

Additionally, by facilitating the benefits strategic planning process, you become privy to every aspect of the client's business plans and operations...pending acquisitions, expansion strategies, workforce plans, etc.

When considering the benefit planning options facing the company, the client looks to you as the acknowledged benefits expert. You have become an insider, a true advisor.

Benefit strategic planning puts you on the same side of the table with both HR and the CFO, at least. This is perhaps the most advantageous – and strategic – service you can offer your clients. Not only can you engage the top executives in a strong advisory role, with benefit strategic planning you can lay the groundwork for future product offerings such as voluntary and health trend management programs. Most important, with benefits strategic planning you build yourself into the client's benefits plan for the next three to five years. And you can charge a handsome fee for the privilege! This is one service that easily establishes your agency's value in a fee-based model.

There is a program that I recommend to my private consulting clients that provides step-by-step guidance to greatly reduce your learning curve on benefits strategic planning but, ultimately, this is a consultative service that you provide your clients in a very hands-on fashion. (See **www.DOorDIEthebook.com** for a list of recommended resources.) Do not leave this powerful solution out of your agency toolbox.

Defined contribution plans

As I mentioned in Chapter 1, there is a strong likelihood that a large number of small employers will discontinue their employer-sponsored group health plan and send their employees to the state or federal exchange for guaranteed-issue health insurance.

Of course, after paying the per-employee penalty for not offering group insurance, the employer will have at least several thousand dollars left per employee that previously had been paying for the employee's health insurance. What to do with that money?

Some employers will keep it all and send it to the bottom line. Others, wiser and more beneficent, will give all or most of it to their employees to purchase insurance from the exchange. This is your opportunity.

You can assist the employer in moving from defined benefit plan sponsorship to a defined contribution (DC) plan. While these terms are common in employee retirement plan discussions, they are returning to the benefits discussion after lying dormant for 20 years or so.

In a DC plan the employer can determine the amount of money he can afford to spend on benefits and control that budget, without any danger of medical inflation driving up his benefit costs. Employees get greater control and more ownership of their benefits spending decisions.

And defined contribution plans offer tax advantages around the benefit spend for both employers and employees even after the end of employer-sponsored group insurance. Employers can make tax-free contributions through health reimbursement arrangements (HRA). Employees can purchase their benefits using tax-free money using premium reimbursement arrangements. And unlike employer-sponsored health plans, there is no minimum contribution and no minimum participation.

You can help the employer both set up a defined contribution plan and communicate the plan to employees as a stand-alone, fee-based service or provide it as a no-charge value-add as part of your overall service offering to justify your consulting fee.

(Check **www.DOorDIEthebook.com** for recommended resources to get your producers trained on DC consulting.)

Either way, your opportunity is huge. Stating "U.S. health care reform sets in motion the largest change in the post World War II era,"[12] the consulting firm McKinsey projects that upwards of 60 percent of educated employers plan to pursue alternatives to offering employer-sponsored health insurance, including "defined contribution"[13] This resembles the massive movement from defined contribution pensions to 401(k)s. Now that promises to be a pretty good opportunity.

Retirement products

Speaking of 401(k)s, retirement products and services represent another great opportunity for benefits agencies. While 401(k)/403(b)/457 plans are not highly lucrative, they do provide meaningful revenue. Moreover, selling retirement plans help you, as the client's advisor, provide two important services.

---

[12] Singhal, Shubham, p. 2.
[13] *Ibid.*p. 6.

First, as HR departments and office managers become more overworked and stressed, having fewer vendors to deal with becomes a tremendous benefit, reducing the number of contacts and meetings needed to conduct business. By becoming more of a one-stop shop for your clients and offering retirement products, your agency can help clients consolidate and shorten their vendor list...and get paid for it.

Second, as benefits agencies seek to provide more value to employers and employees, it's worth noting that employees are increasingly looking to their employer for not only financial products but also financial advice. MetLife's national survey of employees reported that 51 percent of employees expressed interest in "getting advice about investing their retirement funds" through their employer.[14] While there are fiduciary and liability concerns, an advisor can structure an employee education plan around retirement investing and financial issues that will avoid any problems while providing tremendous value to employees and supporting the employer's benefits education mission.

While adding retirement products to your portfolio does require earning or hiring the necessary security licenses, the advantages can easily outweigh the costs and effort.

Property & casualty

While many benefits shops started out as P&C agencies, they quickly discovered the synergies and cross-selling opportunities that a benefits practice offered. Moreover, being a full-service agency providing both the employee benefits and the risk management can have a tremendous impact on retention.

With a need for new revenue streams and profit centers, benefits agencies can return the favor and expand into property and casualty. This presents a ready cross-sell opportunity as well opens a second front in prospecting, giving producers another value proposition and set of solutions to carry into a prospect meeting.

Additionally, the personal lines side of the business offers a doorway into the individual health market, should PPACA push large numbers of employees out of employer-sponsored plans. Everyone has to have auto and homeowners insurance, making for a ready client pool to which your agency could market individual health plans and supplemental health and life products.

---

[14] MetLife, *Seventh Annual Study of Employee Benefits Trends*, 2009.

While it might make sense to start a P&C practice from scratch, it likely would be easier and certainly faster to enter the market through acquisition. With the high number of P&C agency owners looking for the exit due to the aging of the Baby Boomers, you might find several acquisition opportunities in your market.

Third-party solutions

There are many other services you can offer from third party providers. There are many third-party vendors that are using broker distribution for a broad range of solutions extremely useful to HR. These either put you in the revenue stream or are priced to allow you to make a very profitable markup. The box below lists some of the most valuable third-party solutions you can bring to a client.

Third-Party HR Solutions

Technology

> Human resource outsourcing (HRO) services (e.g., payroll) and, specifically, single-source HRO solutions

> Automated online onboarding/perpetual enrollment for new hires

> Consolidated billing

> Employee benefit portals

> Benefits administration systems

> Human resource information systems (HRIS)

Services

> Wellness & employee population health trend management (covered in the next chapter)

> Medication therapy management (MTM)

> Compliance services to help companies meet state & federal regulations on data security & identity theft

> Telemedicine

> Employee benefit ("hidden paycheck") statements

> ➤ Dependant eligibility audits
>
> ➤ Professional employer organization (PEO)
>
> ➤ Employment tax credit (WOTC) services

(Visit **www.DOorDIEthebook.com** for a list of recommended resources and vendors.)

NOTE: Chapter 7 will discuss how a voluntary benefit enrollment can provide many of these solutions to your HR client at no hard-dollar cost.

Playing offense with payroll services

Payroll services can be a highly strategic tool in your portfolio, both to obtain new accounts and to protect the accounts you already have.

In one of the most troubling trends in employee benefits, national payroll providers such as ADP and Paychex are moving into the benefits space with their own brokerage services. These companies seek to leverage their key role as payroll vendor into a much more lucrative role as broker of record on the employee benefits.

To go on the offensive and preempt the payroll giants, brokers can license a payroll service that both generates a steady revenue stream and keeps the payroll companies out of your accounts. Moreover, some payroll services also offer an extensive range of HR outsourcing solutions, providing you with a particularly strong value prop and differentiating you from the competition.

Compliance services

Finally, I want to discuss compliance support services. You probably already assist your clients with compliance around COBRA and their 5500 reporting. But the compliance picture for employers is about to get ugly.

In Massachusetts, the regulatory and compliance burden of the state's healthcare reform – the primary model for PPACA – has required benefits agencies to take on a major portion of the compliance work for their clients as a value-added service for no additional charge. Pat Haraden, principal of Boston-based agency Longfellow Benefits, has had to add two additional staff just to keep their clients compliant with the new regulations.

According to a senior vice president at a leading carrier, a recent study on the paperwork requirements of PPACA concluded that companies with fewer than 100 employees would not have the manpower to remain compliant with the new requirements. PPACA's penalty for non-compliance is $100 per day... per employee... uncapped. Simply put, the penalty for non-compliance could put many small businesses out of business. A company with just 35 employees fined for only three months of non-compliance would face a penalty of around $320,000. Furthermore, with the decreased staffing and do-more-with-less mandate that HR departments are facing, even mid-market companies will be struggling to meet the compliance requirements of PPACA.

I write this for two reasons. As I mentioned earlier, some services you offer without compensation simply because they strengthen your relationship with the client and provide stickiness. Help with PPACA compliance may become one of these. If so, however, it greatly will help you make the case for your fee to the client when it comes time to move to a fee-for-service model. Whatever technology investment you might have to make and the actual staff time required to keep that client compliant – plus a markup for your profit – simply adds to the total value you are bringing the client, justifying a larger fee.

But, I see an opportunity beyond providing compliance support as a no-cost value-add. Due to the onerous compliance burden that PPACA is about to place on employers and due to the client's unfamiliarity with the new regulations, the benefits agency that gets out ahead of the process should be able to offer this compliance service for a fee. The key to my mind is to roll out a turnkey compliance service to clients and prospects *now*.

You can see how a turnkey "PPACA Compliance Program" is different than just doing a bunch of tedious paperwork for the client. The former is viewed as a unique and very high-value service while the latter is perceived merely as hourly labor, your staff doing paperwork instead of the client's staff. This difference in perception is due, in large part, to your knowledge of the law's arcane rules and regulations; if the client doesn't have to learn them in the first place, your value and your client retention both increase.

But this does require that someone on your staff – currently or a new hire – be capable of researching the law and monitoring Health and Human Services for their regulatory decisions and revisions. You may want to hire a compliance specialist to run your turnkey compliance program. There are, of course, law firms and other companies that, for a fee, will provide you with much of this information and keep you current with regulatory changes. But if you don't get ahead of the curve now and make compliance a service your clients pay for, you may end up having to subscribe to the PPACA information service while giving away your compliance services.

Either way, compliance services are an ideal way you can leverage PPACA to provide greater value to your clients.

Pain of disconnect

Payroll and compliance services are a prime example of ongoing services you can provide the client that create what is known as "pain of disconnect" if the service is ended. These services are difficult and troublesome to replace and usually are made available only to your current clients. In other words, if you're fired as the broker, the client loses the service.

These services are of particular value to an agency because the client's desire to avoid the disruption and hassle of replacing the service can increase your retention substantially. Other examples besides payroll are benefit administration/HRIS systems, online perpetual enrollment systems, online benefit communication programs, Work Opportunity Tax Credits (WOTC) services, and automated employee onboarding systems.

The greater the number of resources you can bring to bear on the client's problems, the more successful you will be in solving problems, becoming indispensible, and evolving into your clients' "trusted advisor."

America's health care system is in crisis precisely because we systematically neglect wellness and prevention.

—Tom Harkin

6

Putting Wellness and Health Trend Management in Your Toolbox

I n the MetLife Broker and Consultant Study, half of all brokers and consultants (and almost 60 percent of those in the large group market) reported that they intended to become more involved in providing their clients with health and wellness programs. Excellent idea.

Bending the cost curve

Some of the most innovative brokers already are helping their clients implement aggressive wellness programs to bend the client's medical cost curve by modifying employee behavior.

Wellness? Well, where are the results?

Workplace wellness has been given renewed emphasis by PPACA's wellness measures. But, until recently, most wellness programs have been long on promises and short on measureable ROI. Employers rarely see meaningful impact on health care costs.

Wellness programs fail to reduce health costs because most are "process-only" plans that reward employees for participating in the program, regardless of the results.

More and more employers are asking how they can take their wellness program to the next level, to produce measureable results that drive down health care costs and create a sustainable benefits plan.

Wellness with teeth

The most progressive brokers are moving employers into aggressive "results-based" wellness plans, which require employees to demonstrate results if they want to earn discounts or avoid surcharges on their medical premiums. Results-based programs have been proven to deliver meaningful ROI, actually bending the employee health trend and, by extension, bending the employer's medical utilization and cost curves in a positive direction.

These results-based plans, what I call "wellness with teeth," are effective because they focus on results and monetize wellness incentives to modify employee behavior. (For recommended vendors see the resources list at **www.DOorDIEthebook.com**)

Employers are asking how to structure wellness incentives that both are legal and have the greatest impact to change employee behavior.

Good-driver discount

Results-based programs reward wellness in a variety of ways, such as a reduced payroll contribution, a better health plan, a deductible credit or HRA deposit, or an HSA contribution. These plans generate around 95 percent employee participation!

Employees are asked to think of results-based wellness as a good-driver discount for group health insurance. Employees know that auto insurance costs more if they have a bad driving record and that life insurance costs more if they are a smoker. When the program is explained this way, all employees may not like results-based wellness but they understand and – most important – accept the need for it.

Treating benefits like workers comp

Some employers, and especially HR professionals, often balk at results-based wellness over what they consider punitive and intrusive measures. Employers, however, already impose aggressive and intrusive safety programs to control workers comp costs. When asked why they don't manage their far more expensive health plan costs in a similar fashion, the light bulb tends to go off.

With results-based wellness, an employer utilizes sophisticated method-ologies to drive employee engagement and to identify, measure, reduce, and manage risk within its employee population.

While wellness tools like biometric testing and Health Risk Assessments (HRA) are well known, less familiar will be such tools as predictive analytics, predictive modeling, risk stratification and premium differential that allow employers to leverage biometric and HRA data. There's not enough space here to explain all the details but I urge you to do some additional research to learn about these powerful tools.

Analytics allow employers to mine disparate data sources – such as bio-metrics tests, plan experience data, absenteeism records, etc. – to present an accurate, fact-based picture. The key point here is that C-Suite executives find factual data actionable and are now willing to take forceful, proactive steps related to managing their employee health trend.

Employee Accountability

Employers are using these tools to increase employee accountability in compliance with the 2008 final HIPPA regulations that have been upheld repeatedly by the courts, most recently in an April 2012 decision by a U.S. District Court in Florida.

Risk stratification enables employers to develop new benefit packages that offer incentives and/or payment for participation in wellness activities and compliance with preventive health measures.

A meaningful bend of the curve

The financial impact of a results-based wellness program is now well documented. In groups as small as 50 lives to very large organizations, re-sults-based wellness has proven that it can improve the employee health trend and, thus, bend the health care cost curve down. The case study nearby is a good example of the meaningful results these programs are bringing.

The case study is not an outlier example. Brokers across the country are using results-based wellness programs to achieve similar results that improve both employees' health and employers' bottom lines.

Results-based wellness programs are powerful tools that actually bend the health cost curve down and create a more affordable and sustainable employee benefits plan. By putting a results-based wellness plan in their toolbox, brokers and their employer clients can get aggressive in addressing the impact of employees' health behavior on benefit costs.

CASE STUDY
Results-Based Wellness Produces... Results

A manufacturer with almost 1,900 employees moved aggressively to implement a results-based wellness program to gain some control over an employee population with a wide range of challenging health behaviors. After just a year of a results-based wellness program, the employer realized over $500,000 in bottom-line savings.

Although the maximum financial impact on employees was just $50 monthly, the use of financial incentives produced an astounding 99.6 percent employee participation in the wellness program.

The employer tied four wellness categories to financial incentives: Blood Pressure, Tobacco/Nicotine, Cholesterol and Body Mass Index (BMI). A monthly premium contribution penalty was assessed based on results in these four areas. This cost-shifting to more at-risk employees generated "hard-dollar" net savings to the employer of over $200,000 in the first program year.

At the end of the first year, all four incentive categories had improved. This reduced risk produced "soft-dollar" savings to the employer of more than $320,000 in the form of lower claims.

Focus 90% of your time on solutions and only 10% of your time on problems.
—Anthony J. D'Angelo

7

The Voluntary Toolbox

I am devoting an entire chapter to workplace voluntary benefits (WVB) because WVB provides an entire toolbox of solutions by itself. The voluntary toolbox is stocked with not just a broad range of desirable products but also the valuable ancillary services that can be offered as part of a voluntary benefits enrollment. So adding voluntary is a quick and easy way to expand your menu of solutions, add to your resource toolbox, and provide tremendous value to your clients.

With HR departments facing reduced budgets and management pressure to do more with less, these are valuable tools that a broker can bring to the HR client to solve the client's problems while providing a new revenue stream for the agency.

Even clients that previously might have been resistant to a voluntary offering usually are happy to accept voluntary when it solves a painful problem, especially when that solution comes at no hard-dollar cost to the client, since almost all solutions that WVB can provide have no budget impact for the client.

Additionally, given the lingering economic doldrums, worksite voluntary benefits provide perhaps the most logical cross-sell opportunity. These employee-paid benefits can help employers reduce benefit costs and offset benefit takeaways while allowing employees to plug gaps in their benefit plan.

Moreover, cross-selling worksite voluntary benefits is the single most effective and proven way to add new, meaningful revenue to your agency.

How deep is your voluntary revenue stream?

Many producers discount the revenue impact of WVB, to both their firm and their own income, seeing voluntary benefits as producing insignificant "marginal revenue" and not worth the effort. Yet a successful cross-selling initiative can generate substantial commission dollars for both the agency and its brokers.

With a decent book of business, a typical benefits broker easily can earn $100,000 by cross-selling voluntary, even after splitting commissions with his enrollment partner who does all the heavy lifting. An agency with a healthy book can expect to drive upwards of half a million dollars to the bottom line. That's $500,000 in new revenue with no real work required.

With that kind of money at stake, if your producers don't cross-sell WVB to their clients, someone else surely will. And it's unlikely that that another benefits broker will be content with the BOR on *just* the voluntary....

Of course, there are other products and services your agency can sell to generate new revenue. But voluntary is one of the most natural products for a benefits broker to offer.

In the broker's wheelhouse

Unlike some other product and service offerings that are discussed in previous chapters, voluntary benefits are right in the benefit broker's wheelhouse. The most common WVB are health, disability and life benefits, no different in purpose than the medical and ancillary plans brokers offer now. Like major medical and group life and LTD, voluntary benefits are financial protection products, designed to protect employees from the financial risks that every person faces.

I mentioned that WVB can provide valuable solutions for the employer, sometimes with the products themselves but more frequently with the ancillary services of a voluntary benefits enrollment. Let's take a look at the products first.

Before we do, I want to offer a major word of caution:

YOU CANNOT SPREADSHEET WORKPLACE VOLUNTARY BENEFITS.

I simply cannot emphasize this point enough.

Despite the inclination of every benefits broker to do so, spreadsheeting voluntary just doesn't work. The reason is the product complexity of most voluntary products. There is much less standardization and commoditization of voluntary products than their ancillary cousins. As a result, if you spreadsheet you usually are comparing apples to pears...they may resemble but they're not the same. The differences occur both with basic product design and with riders and other usually optional secondary features.

An excellent example is voluntary Accident. While most Accident plans are both indemnity and reimbursement plans, most pay on a schedule of fixed benefits. Within many – but not all – of those plans, there are coverage level options. This difference alone complicates plan comparisons.

At least one carrier, however, offers an Accident plan that does not pay on a schedule of benefits at all but rather pays all medical expenses resulting from an accident up to a specific dollar amount, say $1,500 or $5,000, usually selected by HR to match the employee's medical deductible. So how do you compare this latter Accident plan to all the others? Not on a spreadsheet. The larger difference in the two plan designs has to be weighed by the broker and the client.

Another quick example is Permanent Life. The industry-leading Universal Life product offers several valuable "living benefits" that the insured can access during his lifetime, while the death benefit is preserved at the original purchased face value. Few if any other UL products come close to matching the living benefits this plan offers; spreadsheeting this best-of-breed UL for price with competitors would be misleading and nonproductive.

Selecting the right voluntary benefits for a particular client is usually a more hands-on process, requiring more research and analysis than does the medical and ancillary plans. Just don't spreadsheet them. Please.

So let's take a look at the most popular and most utilized products in the voluntary benefits portfolio.

VOLUNTARY PRODUCTS

As the manufacturer of products, carriers are the best source for in-depth product training on voluntary benefits. I'll offer a brief overview of the most common and popular worksite voluntary products: short-term disability insurance, permanent life, critical illness, cancer, accident, hospital indemnity, and limited medical. I won't bother with Dental and Vision because many agencies already have these in their portfolio and most brokers are familiar with them.

SHORT-TERM DISABILITY

Like group disability plans, voluntary disability insurance (DI) provides eligible employees income protection insurance in the form of benefits that partially replace income lost as a result of a disabling non-occupational accident or illness. Despite some group DI plans that pay only 50 percent of pay, all voluntary DI pays 60 percent of the insured's salary.

Short-term disability (STD) is the most popular voluntary DI product, offered either alone or to fill the gap with a group long-term disability (LTD) plan. Most voluntary STD plans have a six-month benefit period to cover the 180-day elimination period of most LTD plans.

Plan variables may include:

> Combination benefits covering accidents, sickness or both;

> Elimination periods, which are the number of continuous days (beginning with the first day of total disability) before any monthly benefit amount is payable;

> Benefit periods for which monthly income benefits are payable after the elimination period ends (such periods often include choices of 90 days, six months, one year, two years or three years); and

> Portability, depending upon whether the plans are offered on an individual or group chassis.

PERMANENT LIFE INSURANCE

Voluntary life insurance plans allow employers to provide, at no cost to them, life insurance to eligible employees and family members at rates that reflect group economies of scale. Some products offer popular "living benefits" with the death benefit, which can be accessed when health, life and death circumstances require. Considered life insurance, such products allow employees to receive a benefit while living.

Two primary types of life insurance are term life and permanent life, including whole life and universal life.

Term life insurance offers protection for a specified period of time and builds no cash value. If the insured dies during the specified term, policy benefits are paid to the beneficiary. Coverage may be portable and riders for items such as critical illness/total disability, quality of life, increasing death benefits, AD&D and families are often available. Even if the term life coverage is portable, premiums for term life insurance become prohibitive as the insured reaches retirement age.

Permanent life insurance can play a role in meeting current as well as future financial needs, especially paying final expenses. Consisting of a permanent life insurance policy that protects the policyholder through his/her life, permanent life insurance offers a completion of premiums at a predetermined age. Features of permanent life plans include premiums that remain level throughout the life of the policy, guaranteed renewable protection that cannot be reduced and accumulated cash values that can be withdrawn (upon the policy's surrender), borrowed against as a loan, annuitized or used to purchase extended or reduced paid-up insurance. Some permanent life plans may also include dividends paid annually and guaranteed cash values. A highly popular permanent life rider is a Long-Term Care benefit that helps pay for medically necessary home health and long-term care.

CRITICAL ILLNESS INSURANCE

Critical Illness (CI, also called Specified Illness) insurance pays a lump-sum benefit to the insured upon the diagnosis of a specified critical illness. Typically the covered illnesses include heart attack, stroke, kidney failure, blindness, paralysis and major organ transplant. Coverage of cancer generally is available as a rider. An insured receives a cash benefit upon the diagnosis of the critical illness regardless of what other insurance may pay.

Called "life insurance for people who survive" serious illness, Critical Illness insurance is designed to protect the insured's finances from unreimbursed costs such as co-payments, deductibles, experimental treatments, and more. Many of these expenses will be for non-medical costs such as travel for specialized treatment, ramps & other home modifications, rehabilitation and childcare. In addition to the indirect medical costs there is the loss of income. An insured may have a long-term disability income policy but may have a 90 or 180 day elimination period before benefits will be paid or may not have enough disability coverage. Additionally, a working spouse forfeits all pay when taking time off work to care for their spouse. A Critical Illness policy may be sold as an individual policy or on a group chassis.

Critical Illness insurance works well with high-deductible plans and most are HSA compatible.

With the growing popularity of Critical Illness on a group chassis, guaranteed issue of $5,000 to $15,000 is becoming common with both group and individual chassis product. Benefit amounts typically range from $5,000 to $100,000, with $50,000 being the most common face amount maximum.

CI policies are often sold with an employer-selected wellness rider, which typically pays the insured $50 annually for any one of a wide range of preventative tests such as mammogram, pap smear, stress test, and PSA. For employees 18-29, the wellness payment will offset the annualized premium for a $5,000 CI policy.

CANCER INSURANCE

Despite the growing popularity of Critical Illness insurance, Cancer insurance remains a popular and top-selling voluntary product.

The original design was a scheduled benefit policy with specified dollar benefits for each potential expense. For example, a policy may specify that the carrier will pay the actual charges up to $300 per day for chemotherapy. This remains the most common Cancer plan design.

Influenced by the new CI policies, many carriers during the 1990s began to offer Lump-Sum Cancer policies. These policies pay the face amount upon the diagnosis of internal cancer. Benefit amounts on a Lump-Sum Cancer plan may range from $10,000 to $100,000.

ACCIDENT INSURANCE

Offering protection beyond basic health coverage, voluntary accident insurance provides supplemental on- or off-the-job coverage and may cover deductibles and other services standard health care coverage may not provide. Most voluntary accident insurance products are both a reimbursement and an indemnity insurance policy – expense reimbursements paid are for actual charges or up to the maximum amount stipulated per selection on the Schedule of Benefits.

While most Accident plans pay on from a Schedule of Benefits, some carriers are offering Accident plans that provide a lump-sum benefit, paying accident-related medical expenses up to the benefit amount for any single accident. The benefit amount usually ranges from $1,000 to $5,000 and is designed to match up with the deductible on the group medical. With this type of accident plan, employees have seamless coverage to protect them from the financial risk of out-of-pocket medical expenses due to an accident.

Accident plans are guaranteed issue and premiums for employee-only coverage can be as inexpensive as $3-4 per week. Accident plans are extremely popular with active adults and younger families with children.

Embedded benefits of accident insurance may include:

- Emergency Room benefit;
- Ambulance benefit;
- Hospital confinement;
- AD&D benefit;
- Coverages including off-the-job only or 24-hour coverage; and
- Optional benefits/riders such as accident total disability, hospital intensive care, sickness hospitalization, coverage for spouse and children, and a wellness benefit similar to that available on CI plans.

HOSPITAL INDEMNITY INSURANCE

These policies pay a cash benefit directly to the insured when admitted to a hospital. With the rising number of uninsured people insurance companies have added benefits to these policies to make them more attractive. In addition to a daily hospital benefit that can range from $200 per day in-hospital to as much as $4,000 per day, there may be an immediate separate benefit upon admission to a hospital as well as benefits for in-hospital doctor visits. Other covered expenses may include in and outpatient surgery, diagnostic testing, annual wellness exams and outpatient doctor visit reimbursement.

NON-TRADITIONAL VOLUNTARY PLANS

In addition to these more common voluntary benefits, there is a wide selection of more specialized, non-traditional WVB products, including:

- Limited medical plans;
- Long-term care insurance;
- Personal lines coverage (home/auto);
- Legal plans;
- Identity theft plans;
- Pet insurance;
- Financial wellness;
- Payroll deduction loans;
- Vacation & travel programs; and
- Employee purchasing plans.

While the traditional voluntary benefits will continue to be the mainstays of voluntary programs due to their broad appeal, high utility and robust commissions, these others can be useful additions to a benefit plan, providing valuable benefits to employees and revenue to the broker.

Additionally, because they are portable and follow the employee, voluntary benefits give employees increased financial security in the face of continuing job insecurity.

WVB as a service play

Most brokers overlook the substantial value to their clients of the benefit communication and ancillary services that the voluntary enrollment can provide to solve serious HR problems.

The substantial commission revenue that WVB can generate can be used as a funding mechanism for valuable solutions for HR. And because face-to-face enrollment meetings with a benefit counselor are necessary for high participation in the voluntary offering, a voluntary enrollment provides for highly valuable one-on-one interaction with employees to accomplish HR goals, such as explaining an HSA/HRA or a benefits statement or conducting a survey.

In addition to bilingual enrollment like we saw in the case study in the Section Two introduction and results-based wellness described in the case study in Chapter Six, there are many other services that a voluntary enrollment can provide the client to solve a myriad of HR problems:

> Moving from paper to electronic enrollment of the core benefits;

> Improved communication (and employee appreciation) of the benefits package, core and voluntary benefits;

> Personalized benefit (hidden paycheck) statements;

> Dependant eligibility audits;

> Automated online self-service onboarding; and

> Employee surveys

Any of these could be a solution that gets HR to open the door to a WVB offering. Plus, these solutions are ideal to lead with in lieu of the typical pitch to help the prospect save money on the medical plan.

When you consider that most of these value-added services can be provided at *no hard-dollar cost*, you can understand the powerful competitive edge that WVB can provide the progressive benefit broker. Not only can the broker show the client innovative solutions to HR problems, he can also make the solution available with no impact on the company's budget. That makes for a very strong value proposition, one that can help the broker gain tremendous favor with the client.

While the 21st Century Agency has a wide variety of products and services to choose from for its portfolio, voluntary benefits are the most lucrative and high-value addition an agency can make to its toolbox.

Section THREE

21st Century Marketing
Repositioning Your Agency through High-ROI Marketing

Without promotion, something terrible happens...Nothing!
—P. T. Barnum

Like it or not, change is inevitable. And never before has that been truer for the benefits agency than now, especially when it comes to marketing your business and attracting new accounts.

Other industries have quickly adapted their marketing and promotional efforts to incorporate more effective marketing strategies and meaningful technology and communication tools. At the same time, many of these industries maintain their focus on the most important aspect of marketing: the development of a long-term relationship with a quality prospect and, ultimately, with a client.

The insurance industry (our employee benefits niche included) has been unbelievably slow to adopt new marketing methods that are now becoming standard or even "old-hat" in related industries like finance and healthcare.

So why has our industry been so slow to change? Well, the reason for the resistance to new promotional and marketing concepts is, frankly, because there's been no need to change. That is, until now. With healthcare reform creating an upheaval and chaos, virtually all aspects of our industry are being forced to adapt to the new reality.

However, healthcare reform is only one component forcing benefits agencies to apply "new-to-them" marketing strategies. Technology, the speed of communication, and the availability of information online are also driving forces behind the need for superior, more transparent, more relationship-focused, more intentional marketing efforts. With all these forces coming together at once, it's difficult for any benefits agency to know where even to begin as they consider retooling and reinventing their agency's marketing activities.

With all that said, this section will give you a complete overview of how to modify your agency's marketing efforts, beginning with some general strategies and moving to more specific tactical solutions.

First, there are certain marketing concepts new to the benefits industry that any principal of a benefits firm needs to adopt to properly position their business and successfully attract new accounts.

On top of those foundational concepts, an agency must consistently and proactively hold its marketing activities and investment accountable by adopting the High-ROI Marketing Model. The days of throwing money around and sponsoring this fundraiser and that golf tournament are over, if you want to, first, survive and then dominate your marketplace.

Finally, I'll be detailing specific methods both online and offline that you can use not only to generate new qualified prospects but also to reengage current clients for additional sales opportunities.

Ultimately, the marketing activities in an agency must be deliberate, tested, monitored, and evaluated at a level never before seen in our industry. Only by implementing effective marketing practices that are held accountable for results will a benefits business be able to achieve higher level success as a 21st Century Agency.

Ninety percent of the success
of any product or service is its
promotion and marketing.
　　—Mark Victor Hansen

8

Six Marketing Concepts for the Post-Reform World

To remain relevant, profitable and, ultimately, capable of dominating their respective markets, benefits agencies are being asked to pioneer a brave new world. Never before has it been necessary for agency leaders to reinvent their overall approach to marketing as they now must. Without embracing the concepts on the following pages, agencies will find themselves struggling to produce new, quality accounts and even more difficulty in hanging on to accounts as competitors will consistently be lurking.

Within this chapter, you'll find six foundational marketing principles that apply to virtually all benefits agencies and can be accepted as best practices within our industry. These concepts will lay the groundwork for the following chapters, where I'll dive into more details on implementing a complete marketing program focused on return-on-investment (ROI) and, then, applying specific tactics to attract new accounts.

The six principles have been broken down into the three categories of Prospect-Focused, Business-Focused and Process-Focused to allow you to clearly understand why, how and where these concepts come into play within a benefits firm.

PROSPECT-FOCUSED PRINCIPLES

The new prospect relationship

In all fairness, most agency leaders are masters at developing personal and meaningful client relationships with key decision makers. However, that's not the relationship I'm discussing here. Instead, let's examine the perception that a prospect has of the benefits firm, itself, in a given market, not the personal relationship with the principal or producer.

The questions to ask are these:

➢ What position does your benefits firm hold in the mind of a prospect?

➢ How does the prospective client view your firm?

➢ Will that prospect think of your benefits firm when the time is right?

In other words, do your prospects see your firm as an advisor and true leader in the marketplace or merely as a company that brokers insurance plans? Surprisingly, this critical question of positioning is an often overlooked.

Marketing professionals refer to the idea of positioning as "owning mental real estate." How much mental real estate does your benefits agency own currently in the minds of your prospects and more importantly, how valuable is that real estate?

The most obvious space to compete over is around "benefits." Certainly, this is valuable but, in today's post-reform world, those agencies that primarily and, perhaps, even solely focus on "benefits" will become extinct.

In fact, from a positioning and marketing standpoint, benefits agencies really need to strive to become perceived in the minds of their prospects and clients as advisors on much more than just benefits.

This idea of repositioning your benefits agency and developing a new kind of relationship with prospects can be illustrated by taking a concept from marketing legend, Jay Abraham. In his book, *Getting Everything You Can Out Of All You've Got*, Jay describes the difference between customers and clients:

Customer – Someone who buys something (a *transactional* relationship).

Client – Someone who is under the guidance and protection of a trusted advisor (a *transformational* relationship).

So what do customers and clients have to do with The New Prospect Relationship? Well, in the new world of benefits, the best way to turn a worthy prospect into a client is to treat your ideal prospects as actual clients.

Find ways to provide service, information, useful solutions, etc., even before a prospect actually becomes a full-fledged client. Yes, the lines between a prospect and client will become blurred, and that's not only okay, it's advised!

If you can invest in the mental real estate of your most ideal prospects to have them perceiving your firm as a the preeminent option for them, then the process of attracting new clients and turning them into valuable accounts will happen virtually automatically.

In other words, begin a meaningful, client-like, transformational relationship with your clients while they are still just your prospects, and you'll be well able to dominate your competition.

Quality vs. quantity

Closely related to the concept of developing The New Prospect Relationship, is the idea that you should NOT see every employer as a potential client of your firm.

Some agency leaders have already adopted this principle, understanding that the best way to achieve the highest levels of success in a post-reform world is not by trying to be all things to all businesses.

Similarly, it's critically important also to realize (even in the face of common business dogma) that significant success will not be achieved by trying to do just one thing the best and offering it to everyone.

So, if a benefits agency should not be all things to all people and it shouldn't focus on just one thing for all people, what should it do?

Simply put, benefits agencies should be many (not all) things for its highest quality (not all) prospects.

Thus, we come to the main point. Now and in the future, the most successful agency leaders will be focused on the quality of prospects rather than the quantity of prospects.

The fact is, your agency's current situation, capacity, personnel, portfolio, size, clients, etc. all must be considered when determining which prospects are the best ones for your business. Even prospects that represent more potential bottom line dollars may not be the ones you should focus on attracting.

In our work with agencies, we often find them targeting prospects primarily on group size, i.e., number of employees. While that is an important aspect of prospect quality, it's only one of many that should be considered including industry, location, current benefits situation, business model, etc.

As entrepreneurs, it's unnatural for us to disqualify prospects and that often makes this is a difficult principle to apply. However, the more targeted you are with your prospects, the more effective you will be at attracting them through your positioning and marketing activities. Yes, sometimes this may mean you don't go after the new large business that every other agency in town is chasing.

More profitably, this principle allows you always to know what prospects you specifically want to work with and which ones you don't. You'll never again have to worry about wasting time on prospects that you're not likely to successfully turn into clients anyway.

BUSINESS-FOCUSED PRINCIPLES

Marketing & sales integration

Unfortunately, many benefits firms view marketing as a completely separate activity from everything else in the organization. Specifically, leaders often see marketing and sales as two separate activities that are hardly related. Now more than ever, it's vital that agency leaders realize that marketing must be completely integrated into every other aspect of the firm, especially sales.

This does not mean marketing takes over; it simply means that marketing is elevated to the level of importance and intentional decision making it deserves for the firm to be as profitable as possible. Often, the activities of promotion, positioning, and prospect communication are reactions to the current situation rather than part of a proactive, holistic, strategic and deliberate plan. Just as sales activity should be driven by a systematic process, so should your marketing activity.

Sales leaders should meet consistently with marketing leaders. Successes and failures should be shared amongst the departments of the firm, specifically between sales and marketing. Proactive, thoughtful marketing activity produces easier, faster and more profitable sales results.

Consider a metaphor from the military. When an attack is about to begin, the attacking force first softens up the opposing forces on the ground through bombing raids, artillery and the like to reduce the enemy's resistance.

This way, the attacking ground troops will have a much easier time completing their mission of taking more and more ground from the enemy.

Put aside the idea of you being an "attacker" and your prospect being the "enemy," even though some days it may feel exactly like that. Instead, focus on the meaning of the metaphor. Your agency's marketing efforts (bombing and artillery) should be designed to soften up the prospect for your ground troops (producers) so that the selling process is a natural evolution of the prospect relationship, rather than a fork in the road that everyone knows is coming and somewhat dreads. The producer fears the failure of not closing the sale, whereas the prospect fears being sold, having to reject someone or making the wrong decision whether a "yes" or "no."

Ultimately, the integration of marketing and sales is not a revolutionary idea; it's an evolutionary idea that more and more industries have increasingly begun to adopt. In the brave new world of benefits, this integration is a core principle that will serve your agency well.

Marketing as an equity builder

Many agency principals have considered or are considering selling their business, either now or later. For most, this is a natural exit strategy. However, in the post-reform world, the valuation of a benefits business has changed significantly. With commission compression and the continuing erosion of medical commissions, the firm is most likely worth not nearly what it was worth before 2010. Thus, to restore that higher valuation, firms must find other ways to increase the equity value of the business.

Marketing provides a path to building more equity in any benefits firm. This is not a particularly new concept in most industries and benefits agencies can implement similar value-building marketing strategies, as well.

Specifically, successful marketing gives a firm two crucial ways to build its equity. First, and most obviously, the more successful your marketing, the more clients you have, and thus, the greater your firm's equity overall. Second, by developing a proven marketing approach and then systematizing it with tools, scripts, plans, checklists, etc., you create a very valuable business development asset that an acquiring firm would find very attractive.

While these ideas are simple, they are important, and potentially can allow you to continue to notch up the value of this aspect of your business. For you, selling your firm may not be an end goal but regardless, understanding that the proper approach to marketing will lead to a more stable, viable and profitable firm should be benefit enough to actively optimize your marketing efforts.

PROCESS-FOCUSED PRINCIPLES

Measuring marketing success (and failure)

In the good old days, (you know, back in the 90s and early 2000s and certainly before) benefits firms were able to spend marketing dollars that were not accountable for directly producing a positive return-on-investment. Instead, those dollars were used in more abstract ways, such as sponsorships and general brand advertising. While there is a time and place for such marketing methods, if benefits agencies continue to not hold their marketing dollars accountable, they will quickly find smaller, smarter, marketing-savvy firms outpacing and dominating them.

In today and tomorrow's world, there is and will continue to be less margin for error. Playing around with a marketing budget by sponsoring the golf tournament or a hosting table at the community fundraising gala simply will not get the job done. These aren't effective marketing expenditures; they are better characterized as charitable donations. Again, I'm not suggesting those expenditures do not have a place but they must be pulled back and those dollars reallocated into activities that can be measured and modified as needed.

Producer sales results usually are measured relatively well within a benefits firm. However, the effectiveness of a given marketing strategy is rarely ever measured. The primary reason for this is that most marketing done by benefits firms cannot be measured. And that creates a problem.... Without measurement, when marketing is ineffective, no one realizes it. Thus, the marketing expenditures continue on month after month, year after year without producing any significant results, and certainly without producing a positive return-on-investment. Those dollars go down the drain and are completely wasted.

As you know, if you don't measure it, you can't manage it. Thus, every time a marketing strategy is used that cannot be measured, there's no hope for being able to effectively manage it or improve its outcome. Investing in marketing efforts that cannot be or are not measured represents one of the most substantial wastes of resources within our industry today. Only by truly reinventing this aspect of your firm's marketing will you be able to continue to compete in the future.

Put succinctly, results must rule the day.

Brand-building vs. direct communication

I alluded to this idea in the previous discussion on measuring your marketing. Here, I want to be more direct and specific with what measurable marketing activities are and are not.

Let me begin by defining the two general styles of marketing.

The first and more easily recognized is brand-building, also called image-building or brand-imaging. Regardless of its name, branding (as I'll refer to it) focuses on making sure the masses know who your firm is. Branding usually puts attention on the business name, logo and slogan. For instance, the hypothetical Wilson Benefits Firm may have a billboard in the primary business district of their city that says, "Wilson Benefits Firm – The Best Solutions & Service for Employers Since 1957" along with their branded logo.

Examples of branding from other industries bombard us everyday on television, on the radio, in our mail, and, of course, online in ads and our email. Coca-Cola, Verizon, McDonald's, etc. all depend upon multi, multi-million dollar marketing campaigns to continue reminding the masses they still exist, sometimes offering new products and services but always focusing on their image and brand.

A brand is an incredibly important asset for any business but it's especially critical for a company that depends upon the masses and a massive market share to continue its growth and profitability.

Direct marketing

The second style of marketing is built around direct communication with a select few. Known as direct-response marketing or direct marketing, this style focuses on developing irresistible or enticing offerings and then, putting those offers in front of the most qualified, targeted prospects – the most ideal prospects for that business. These prospects are asked to respond in very specific ways to the offers and, in so doing, two marvelous things happen 1) a prospect has chosen to engage with the business and 2) the prospect's response is measurable because it can be tracked. Therefore, direct marketing automatically fulfills the need of measuring marketing results.

While there are fewer common examples to point to because of the targeted nature of direct marketing, look at the direct mail you receive or emails you get from companies you've bought from in the past. Most often, those media will make an offer specifically to you. Infomercials are another very obvious example of direct-response marketing. These paid programs air at specific times of day on specific channels in order to reach a specific, intentionally chosen and targeted audience. Amazon has been and continues to grow its direct marketing capabilities. When you make a product selection on Amazon, they automatically make recommendations to you based on your current searches and past buying history. This is a real-time and very powerful form of direct marketing.

Direct marketing is most often observed in business-to-consumer industries because we're all consumers. However, this marketing style can be just as effective used in business-to-business industries where it often is dismissed out of hand or simply ignored because "it's not what everyone else is doing."

In the post-reform world, a successful benefits agency MUST do things that are "not what everyone else is doing." Thus, while certain aspects of branding have their place, direct marketing should become the default style of positioning and promotion for a benefits agency.

The simple truth is this...

➤ A benefits firm does not need to waste valuable resources trying to market to the masses nor should it. Instead, it should choose its ideal prospects and communicate primarily with them.

➤ A benefits firm receives very little measurable return-on-investment from branding activities. Instead, it should employ methods that are able to be tested and improved by measuring success and failure and adapting accordingly.

➤ A benefits firm achieves no meaningful prospect engagement through a branding message. Instead, it needs to engage prospects in interesting and interactive ways, which direct marketing can provide.

The reality about direct marketing is that you are building your brand at the same time. Each time you put a valuable offer in front of a targeted prospect, they also see and internalize your brand. Thus, direct marketing allows you to meaningfully engage a prospect, get them to respond to you, and build your brand simultaneously.

To that point, I'd like to end this discussion with a quote from master marketer Lenny Lieberman, the man responsible for marketing multiple million- and billion-dollar product lines, including the now famous Pro-Activ skin care system:

Always brand while you sell, never before you sell. Brand building should be the by-product of your marketing, not the primary objective.

As I close out this chapter, I trust you realize the necessity of these six principles and how they will aid in your efforts to reinvent your agency into one can survive and profit in the face of health reform.

These marketing principles are already at work in the some of the most successful benefits firms and they have been used by leading businesses across many industries. It's time to adopt them and let them guide your marketing efforts to a bigger bottom line.

You need the kind objectivity that makes you forget everything you've heard, clear the table and do a factual study like a scientist would.

—Steve Wozniak

Plug the Marketing Drain
The High-ROI
Marketing Model

With benefits agencies across the country dealing with massive changes and challenges presented by reform, it is critical you subscribe to the most efficient, effective and accountable marketing practices to ensure positive and predictable growth.

The concept of the marketing drain and the five-step High-ROI Marketing Model will give you a solid, proven plan to apply that delivers a consistent and predictable high return-on-investment and simultaneously prevents significant financial resources from going down the drain.

To begin, it's critical that you understand the very real marketing drain and why it is detrimental to any benefits agency, especially as margins continue to slim and every dollar becomes even more valuable.

So what is the marketing drain?

The Marketing Drain – A costly condition that wastes agency resources (manpower & money) due to your failure to measure results and hold your marketing accountable.

Notice that not only dollars but also another very valuable resource, manpower, goes down the drain. Between wasted labor and cash, it's obvious just how much of a liability the marketing drain can become to a benefits firm. Of course, it's also important to point out that besides the lost resources, there is also the opportunity costs faced by squandering assets. What successes could have been created with those assets had they not been wasted?

Naturally, once you accept the idea of the marketing drain, the question becomes, how can an agency leader plug that drain to get the most out of every resource?

Here's the answer...

The ONLY Way to Consistently, Predictably Create Growth and Profit Over the Long-Term Is to Utilize a System that Holds Your Marketing Investment Accountable So You Can Take **CERTAIN & SUCCESSFUL** Actions Based on Real World Results.

Thus, we come to The High-ROI Marketing Model....

The model is made up of a five step process that provides a comprehensive treatment for any benefits agency's marketing activity. Most importantly, this model provides a way to stop using hope and guesswork to achieve actual real-world results. Finally, the program is not overly complicated to implement.

Before we get into the five specific steps, let me offer up a definition for what I mean when I use the term High ROI Marketing...

High-ROI Marketing – A process that uses direct-response marketing strategies that have been tested, measured and optimized to predictably achieve the highest level of growth and profit and, thus, ROI.

The key word in that entire definition is "predictably." No longer should you be in the dark regarding the effectiveness of your marketing efforts. By developing a marketing system and then consistently refining your marketing activities, you'll have complete control over your prospecting results. Essentially, it comes down to what should become the key axiom for your marketing and prospecting efforts: Do more of what works and less of what doesn't.

With that in mind, let's dive into a straightforward five-step system you can adopt to move closer to having total control over your agency's prospecting efforts.

The High-ROI Marketing System

STEP 1 Determine Your Direction

With any journey, you must first know where you're headed. This is also true with an agency's marketing and prospecting efforts. Without having some essential information to guide your firm's marketing decisions, attracting new accounts will be like grasping at straws. Only by identifying clearly four components will you and your agency be able to maximize your prospecting results. These four components make up the Marketing Success Equation, which will become the ultimate guide for your firm's marketing.

This first step is critical to ensure you get the right start, and because it includes several important concepts that cannot be left out, I've devoted the entire next chapter to detailing this concept. For now, I'll simply provide a high-level overview.

The Marketing Success Equation

Right Market + Right Message + Right Media + Right Time = Marketing Success

I'll quickly give you an explanation of each component before we move on to Step 2. In the next chapter, I'll provide more comprehensive descriptions, giving you some specific thoughts on how you can successfully identify each component for your business.

Right Market – By determining who your ideal prospects are, you can target your market and, thus, position your agency more effectively for that specific group. Think of this element as your "Who."

Right Message – Crafting a powerful core message as well as compelling tactical messages requires you to carefully match your message to your target market. Your Right Message can be considered "What" your firm is marketing.

Right Media – This component simply identifies the best way to put your message in front of your market. Usually, this is where most agency leaders spend too much time. Selecting media is important but it must considered in terms of both your market and your message. In essence, the Right Media is your "How."

Right Time – The final component is "When." Determining the best time to market to your target market throughout the year and developing an ongoing marketing and prospecting calendar is critical to ensure your firm always keeps the pipeline full.

Intentionally choosing these four components for your agency's success is essential if you want to have consistent and ongoing business growth through your marketing efforts. Be sure you read through the next chapter to have a more complete and detailed understanding of these elements and how they work together.

STEP 2 **Reallocate Your Resources**

In order to truly reinvent itself, a benefits agency must apply its resources in new ways. You likely will need to make one of the primary reallocations for the prospecting activities of your agency. Specifically, I'm talking about reallocating your agency's resources from branding efforts to direct marketing efforts.

In order to make this reallocation truly effective and help the rest of your team understand why this is being, I recommend following a straightforward process as follows...

Redefine the Objective of Your Resources – Because most benefits firms do not track or measure their marketing, there is not a stated specific objective of their marketing other than to "get more clients." To become a 21st Century Agency, your business must change that and instead make your objective to produce a positive return-on-investment time and time again. By redefining your objective, you automatically accept the fact that you invest your available resources in direct marketing instead of mere branding.

(On the following page, I provide you a list of the Seven Key Marketing Results that will give you even more specific objectives to achieve.)

Implement Direct Marketing – Now that your firm has refocused the purpose of its marketing, you must actually apply direct marketing to engage your prospects. While you should not try to do too much at once that is new, you should work to try new marketing strategies on a consistent basis. Before long, your agency will have transformed its entire approach to marketing.

Make Decisions on Risk vs. Reward – So how do you select what prospecting strategies and tactics to use? Well, take a page from the book of insurance. Insurance is built on the idea of risk. As you choose marketing methods, select some that are more outside the box and others that are less "risky." Consider the expected reward (return) in terms of the risk. The idea is to use a well-balanced mix of methods. Over time, you should test a wide variety of marketing tactics to find which ones work the best for your firm.

One final cautionary note.... Do not just assume a marketing strategy will work. Instead, roll out your prospecting tactics on a limited basis. Test the waters, so to speak. In Step 5, I'll walk you through a process to follow regardless of how well a strategy works.

The reallocation of resources is a vital step in reinventing your marketing to stop your valuable resources from going down the marketing drain.

The Seven Key Marketing Results

- Identify & clarify the reasons a client will use your service vs. your competition

- Increase your overall number of clients, your client base and your number of lives.

- Lower the cost it takes to acquire a new client.

- Increase your overall (and segmented) marketing return-on-investment.

- Increase the frequency your clients engage your firm and accept your solutions.

- Increase the average transaction size of your clients.

- Increase the total average lifetime value of each client.

STEP 3 Measure Your Metrics

I realize I've mentioned this concept of tracking and measuring your marketing results previously but it is so vital to holding your marketing accountability and your agency's success that it's also an integral part of the High-ROI Marketing System.

Without the ability and willingness to track and measure your marketing, your firm will have no data from which to make educated decisions. Any prospecting activities you decide on would be based on guesswork and a gut feeling. You certainly don't operate other areas of your business based on sheer guesswork, so why would you do so with your marketing?

Logistically, this may seem like a difficult process to implement, especially if you haven't measured your marketing results in the past. In fact, however, it's merely a matter of taking it on and getting the process set up.

The following four activities will help you do exactly that...

Choose Prospecting Methods You Can Measure – This goes without saying. If a particular marketing strategy cannot be tracked and therefore measured, then you should reconsider it. For instance, it is very difficult if not impossible to track and, therefore, measure results from event sponsorships and the like. Thus, those expenditures should be reallocated for prospecting that you can measure.

Implement Tracking Systems – Naturally, the ability to track and measure marketing results does not equate to actually tracking and measuring those results. A benefits firm must think through a particular marketing process and then set-up key points in the process that are tracked either manually or automatically. During the actual marketing process, the focus simply should be on measurement and tracking; analysis will be conducted at a later time.

For instance, if a producer is going to call twenty HR directors in a given week, then as those calls are made, he simply needs to make note (manually or in a CRM) of the outcome of each call. What those results really mean can be determined later.

Know Your Key Metrics – An organization must have key benchmarks it wants to hit in different areas of its business. In order to do so, it must be consistently examining key metrics. In Chapter 18 I'll be discussing ten such metrics that should be monitored. Your firm, however, will most likely have others that are critical and thus, you must ensure you are tracking enough of the right data to be able to determine accurately your success or lack thereof in reaching your established benchmarks.

Measure Each Part of Your Agency as a Profit/Loss Center – Currently, this idea is most likely being implemented on an intuitive level. And while intuition certainly has its place, the idea of examining each element of your firm as a profit/loss center needs to be more scientific. Essentially, you need to know if any given activity (or person) in your business is generating more value than it consumes. In other words, is a given person or aspect of your business worth more than what it costs? "Costs" may refer to dollars but it may also refer to emotional investment, use of time, etc.

Measuring your metrics is a vital step in this process. Without the successful implementation of a tracking system for your marketing data, your firm will wander aimlessly able to offer only a best guess at what actions to take next. To continue the metaphor from the Prologue, this marketing data will become a key part of the map that will allow you to successfully move higher up the mountain.

STEP 4 Review Your Results

Now that a process has been tracked and measured, it's time to give that data meaning by reviewing and analyzing those results. Data that is not properly analyzed represents nothing more than wasted resources. The following activities provide a guide on how you can successfully develop and manage this three-part review process.

Consistently Analyze Performance Results – A critical first step is scheduling routine times for analysis and review of the various data that has been collected. These reviews may need to be completed daily or weekly for certain activities, whereas other data may to be reviewed only monthly or even annually. Schedule time to review each marketing activity, select the appropriate personnel to conduct that review, and hold yourself or your staff accountable for completing it and reporting to you the results.

Define Reasons for Failure & Success – Once meaning has been given to the data, you need to determine the reason for failure or success. The data will most often give you insight into why a specific prospecting practice was successful or not. Sometimes, though, you will have to make inferences. Please note that you should determine reasons for both failure *and* success. Most businesses only examine failures and try to fix them. Reviewing success is just as important, as you may discover a profound reason for the success that you hadn't considered before.

Identify Specific Breakdown Points – Once meaning has been given to raw data and reasons for success or failure have been determined, now it's time to identify specific breakdown points for the marketing strategy. Remember, this is all part of the process to hold your marketing accountable and produce consistent high return-on-investment results. To identify these breakdown points, look through the specific marketing strategy or campaign and determine when the results started going south. More than likely, that will indicate the breakdown point.

To continue our example of a producer calling HR directors from Step 3, if the producer is able to get the directors on the phone but unable to schedule a follow-up meeting, then the breakdown point is most likely within the phone conversation that the producer is having with the director.

That's a simple example and, admittedly, most marketing practices are substantially more complex. But don't make this process more difficult than it needs to be. The key is that you commit your agency to completing it and that it gets done to ensure you're not continuously throwing away valuable marketing dollars.

STEP 5 Correct Your Course

The final step of the High-ROI Marketing System is to take action based on the process you've just completed. If you don't take action after completing all this work, you've essentially wasted additional time, energy and money – the limited resources of any firm.

To fulfill this step of course correction, our team has developed The E.M.O. Model, which actually can be applied in many areas of your business, not only for your marketing and prospect efforts. Ultimately, this model is all about doing more of what works and less of what doesn't, which should be the primary goal for your firm's marketing.

The E.M.O. Model

Eliminate – When you discover a completely failed prospecting practice, and there's no reasonable hope that it could be successful, then you should eliminate it. This can be a difficult decision due to sunk cost, when money and time have been invested. But do not throw good money after bad. Sometimes, even the most seemingly brilliant marketing strategy fails miserably. When that happens, rid it from your agency. Don't let the novelty or the "shiny-ness" of a prospecting tactic blind you or your team from what the data tells you. If it's not getting the results you need, dump it.

Modify – Many times, especially as you try new marketing ideas and practices, you'll find that, while the strategy did not achieve the desired results, it does show some promise. If that's the case, don't automatically remove it from your marketing arsenal. Instead, look at different ways you could improve and modify it so you can roll it out again. Successful marketing is developed by constant testing. So do not be unwilling to try something three, four or even a dozen times so long as it reasonably continues to show improved results.

Optimize – When you have a success and you've determined that the success can be repeated, you should ramp up those effective marketing methods. In short, if a strategy works, use it more. A warning though – just because you had a big success with a strategy once doesn't automatically mean those results will be repeated. Therefore, if you have a good success, celebrate it, and then try it once again. If it is again successful, then you can consider increasing the strategy's scope. Marketing is all about testing different tactics and strategies to continuously improve your results.

The rule is, when in doubt about a prospecting tactic, test, test, test.

In the end, the firm that can best evaluate its marketing failures and successes and then change its tactical direction the quickest will ultimately dominate the marketplace. Making educated, thoughtful changes to your marketing practices quickly and assertively is the hallmark of a agency that is able to outpace the competition and consistently attract new clients.

This is the High-ROI Marketing System. I realize this is a different approach for most benefits agency leaders. I also know that when this program is fully adopted and implemented, it will be a true game-changer for your firm. After all, holding your dollars and resources accountable to produce the best kinds of marketing results cannot be a bad practice.

Right Market + Right Message +
Right Media + Right Time =
Marketing Success
     —Scott Cantrell

10

The Marketing Success Equation

Picking up where I left off early in the previous chapter, here I'll discuss the details of selecting each component of the Marketing Success Equation for your benefits firm.

Especially now that you have a complete explanation of the entire High-ROI Marketing System, you're even better equipped to choose these marketing elements in a way that will let you consistently create successful marketing campaigns and promotions within your marketplace.

As a quick review...

The Marketing Success Equation

Right Market + Right Message + Right Media + Right Time =
Marketing Success

Right Market

As was discussed in the previous chapter, the most successful benefits agencies are narrowing their focus down to their specific ideal prospects. To dominate your market, you must first determine what that market is for your firm. Different characteristics should be considered when you target the right market including: group size, industry, existing clients, geographic location, prospect needs, your available solutions, etc.

It's important to note that you do not need to limit your agency to only one "right market." That said, I wouldn't recommend more than four separate targeted groups of prospects. All this raises the question, how does an agency go about selecting its target markets?

Ironically, asking the right questions is a good first step in answering that question to best select your target market(s). Here are three questions to get you thinking...

What do your current clients have in common? Finding those commonalities will point to the kind of prospects that you're most likely to be successful selling and serving.

What groups/businesses would most benefit from your current (or soon to be added) products and services? It's easy to say that "any" business would benefit from working with your firm but the reality is that certain businesses or industries are most interested in the solutions you provide and would benefit from them more than other potential clients.

With what industries or groups do you or your team have pre-existing relationships or connections? Surprisingly, even your veteran producers and other staff may have unutilized in-roads and connections with potential clients or industries that could be leveraged into opportunities.

Without knowing who you are specifically marketing to and prospecting for, you'll be constantly struggling to get your message to all potential clients, and that is a tremendous misallocation of resources. After all, most will never become your clients in the first place, so why waste time, energy and money marketing to them?

Instead, take some serious time and thought to determine precisely who your target market(s) should be. Then, you can craft the most compelling and effective messaging for those particular prospects, allowing you to dominate that specific target market.

Right Message

As the second component of the Marketing Success Equation, the Right Message is critical to a benefits firm's ability to successfully educate and influence a prospect to work with the firm.

Your agency probably already has some sort of core message. The key question, however, is this, what makes your benefits agency special? What separates you from all the other firms actively working to attract the same prospects? Once you can craft a compelling answer to this question, you'll have a tremendously valuable asset at your disposal.

Crafting such a message or what is called a Unique Selling Proposition (USP) is not something that should be ignored or taken lightly. This core message can be one of your best allies in the marketing process. Below is a simple definition.

Unique Selling Proposition – A simple, short statement that identifies your agency's single biggest point of differentiation and its biggest benefit to its target market.

Here are some questions that will move you closer to developing an effective USP for your firm....

What does your target market(s) really want? Consider the characteristics of your target market(s) and then identify what they need and want most. I'm not talking about specific products and services. I'm talking about the *results* they want. Those results could be less employee turnover, lower operations costs or even just certainty around premium costs (the Holy Grail). Once you've identified those real needs and desires, you'll be well-equipped to craft a compelling message.

How can your agency communicate to prospects that you can fulfill a given desire for them in the best possible way? In other words, you need to demonstrate, either through actions, case studies or client endorsements that you can indeed do what you say you can do.

What promise could you make to your prospects to instantly grab their attention and spark a meaningful conversation? This is the ultimate goal, to create a simple statement that will have the key decision makers saying, "Wow, you can do that?!" With that kind of awed response, you'll have given yourself every chance to turn the prospect into a client.

Arming yourself with a compelling and powerful core message is critical to your firm's prospecting success. As you put it out in front of your target market(s), you'll be able to get more engagement from your most ideal prospects.

Right Media

In today's marketing world, media seems to rule the day. Similarly, when it comes to your benefits agency, media will ultimately determine if your message reaches the right decision makers. Think of media as the vehicle that delivers your firm's message to your target market. The question then becomes, what is the Right Media that will most effectively communicate your Right Message to your Right Market?

A quick disclaimer... When it comes to media selection, it's very easy to suffer from "Shiny Object Syndrome." That is, it's easy to be seduced by the latest and greatest technology and communication toys, thinking they will make a difference. The reality is that, while media selection is important, as with any marketing decision it should not be done impulsively. Instead, media options should be deliberately chosen and used based on the message they are delivering and the market they are trying to reach. Do not fall into the trap of thinking that because you or one of your producers think a certain tool or technology is cool or cutting-edge, that it effectively will achieve its goal.

Media comes in many shapes, sizes and forms, offline and online. Many agency leaders are constantly trying to decide between doing more marketing online or maintaining certain offline marketing activities. The right choice is not between offline and online but rather how much of each. And how much of each depends upon your target market and how they will best receive your marketing message.

Here are the questions to consider regarding media....

To which media do the key decision makers of your target market most often read, watch or listen? Consider who your key decision makers are. Depending on your target market, they may be the owner or it could be the CFO or it could be the HR Director. Each of these folks consume different types of media. Only by knowing who those decision makers are will you be able to best select effective media.

What specific media channels should you use to reach your target market(s)? Print, radio, television, email, search engine optimization, public speaking, direct mail, and educational meetings are all ways you potentially could reach out to your market. Narrow the exhaustive list of media options based on your target market and the message you want to send.

How can you best stand out from your competitors by using creative media? A little creativity will go a very long way in developing new clients. Consider incorporating fun, entertainment, and even a little silliness from time to time in your marketing. Even business owners and CEOs like to have fun and never think for one second they are too sophisticated for "fun." Why do so many businesspeople love to go to a conference in Las Vegas...the heat?

It's easy to get overwhelmed when you consider the hundreds of media options that are available. The secret is in not focusing on all the different media choices but rather on what media your target market is most likely to see and then respond to. Knowing that information makes selecting media a much easier and more profitable activity.

Right Time

When is the best time to prospect for new business? Yes, you're right, the answer is, *all the time*, at least generally speaking. Beyond the realization that your firm must always be prospecting, there are certain strategies related to marketing and timing that you should consider.

When should I reach out to my prospects? Once again, "all the time" is a good answer. However, depending upon your target market, there will certainly be times throughout the year that you should ramp up your prospecting efforts. The secret to this is to consider your prospects' annual calendar and market when they are most likely to be thinking about needing the solutions you provide.

How often should I make an impression on my prospects? As with your clients, you should actively be in front of your prospects on a monthly basis. With your best prospects, you could consider being in front of them weekly, perhaps through an email newsletter that – here's the key – delivers real value.

How does my target market's buying cycle affect our marketing timing? This is very closely related to the first question but is different in that it specifically references the buying process. When do your ideal prospects actually buy? For most, it probably is mid-year but for others it may not be. In fact, you could consider attempting to move clients purposefully to an off-cycle renewal so that you have less competition.

Ultimately, you should develop an annual marketing calendar to provide a framework for your ongoing prospecting activities as well as your marketing campaigns. In this way, you can easily plan ahead and make much more deliberate and intentional decisions related to your Right Market, Right Message and Right Media.

Putting all four components of the Marketing Success Equation together correctly will yield very successful results. Naturally, you most likely will not get all four components right the first, second or even third time you try. The goal should not be perfection but rather consistent improvement that will lead to the development of consistent positive return-on-investment from your prospecting efforts.

The key is not to call the decision maker.
The key is to have the decision maker
call you.
      —Jeffrey Gitomer

11

20 Strategies, Tactics & Tools to Attract New Accounts

Throughout this chapter, I'll be revealing no fewer than twenty different strategies, tactics and tools you can use to attract new, qualified prospects as well create new sales opportunities with your current clients.

Before I get into specifics, let me share some insights that will help you mentally apply these methods as you read through them.

First, all of these concepts can be used in many different ways. At first, I considered categorizing the chapter based on the outcomes that each method produces but it didn't take long to realize that each method can easily be used to achieve different objectives.

For instance, a category of Relationship Builders sounds good but the reality is, all of these methods can and should be used to build a relationship whether with a current or a potential client. Thus, the various strategies, tactics and tools are organized into categories based on the general media they each employ.

Second, maintain an open mind and, instead of dismissing certain methods out of turn, consciously consider how you could use these methods in your agency. Some of them will lend themselves more for your current clients while others are more often used to attract new clients. I mention that so that you will think not only in terms of attracting new clients but also in terms of creating new opportunities with existing clients. After all, your current clients are by far your best prospects and should be treated as such.

Finally, while I'll provide a very wide variety of methods here, this list is by no means exhaustive or anywhere close. The concepts I'll lay out here are proven prospecting and marketing methods, many of which have come directly from successful benefits agencies that have implemented them with great results. All of these methods have their place but I can't necessarily recommend out of hand implementing all of them for your agency. Consider this list as an smorgasbord of sorts where you can pick and choose the strategies, tactics and tools that will deliver positive results for your firm.

There are six general categories I'll move through to give you a "marketing arsenal" for your benefits agency that I'm confident can and will serve you well.

Prospecting Tools

When someone thinks about marketing or prospecting, probably the most common type of methods that come to mind are prospecting tools like the ones I'll describe here. While you may be familiar with some or even all of these tools, I'm confident that you'll see them in a new light as you read through the explanations.

And yes, there are literally dozens and even hundreds of possible prospecting tools your firm could use. The ones you'll see here provide benefits agencies the most positive impact most of the time.

Profiles of Success Book - This one strategy, while it may take a little effort to put it together, could become one of the most effective marketing and selling tools your agency possesses. A Profiles of Success Book is simply a collection of positive feedback, testimonials, endorsements and case studies from your current clients. The book (or booklet if preferred) is mailed, emailed and/or shown to your prospective clients and even can be given to them if you choose to do so. As the prospect reads page after page of testimonials, it won't take them long to decide they want to work with you. After all, all those clients praising your work can't be wrong.

Client Newsletter – A monthly newsletter is considered by most marketing professionals, regardless of industry, to be the best overall marketing tool. And while most businesses settle for sending out simply an email newsletter, they are missing out on the vast benefits that are created with a mailed hardcopy newsletter. Because this is such a critical tool for you to employ, I'm going to go into more detail.

A monthly client newsletter...

Makes an impression. Virtually none of your competitors will be sending out a newsletters written for their key decision makers (HR directors, CFOs, CEOs, etc.) so you can easily and instantly position yourself and your agency ahead of them. Every month when your clients get a tangible, printed newsletter, they will realize that you truly are adding value and investing in an ongoing relationship with them.

Builds an ongoing relationship. Through your newsletter, you'll be communicating in a fun, personal way to your clients month after month. Your newsletter should NOT only be about valuable insurance issues and other HR solutions; it also should include jokes, human interest stories, lifestyle tips, etc. In this way, you keep your clients engaged and referring to your newsletter all throughout the month.

Creates expectancy. Each month, your clients will grow to expect your newsletter. Imagine your best prospects (your clients) expecting to receive a message from you every single month. This is exactly what happens when you begin sending a newsletter. Who do you think they'll continue to do business with and refer to their friends with this kind of expectancy?!

I encourage you to begin sending a hardcopy newsletter out to your key decision makers and discover the kind relationships it can help you develop. Yes, you can and should also send out an email version but there's still something meaningful about holding a tangible document in your hands and paging through it, so absolutely use a hardcopy version.

(For a list of recommended client newsletters that automate the entire process, go to **www.DOorDIEthebook.com**.)

Employee Newsletter – While the concept is the same as a client newsletter, this newsletter has a different target. During a benefits conference, Scott was delivering a presentation to leading agency principals and asked this question, "How have you directly been in contact with those people who ultimately are the end users of the solutions you provide?" Of course, he was referring to what we call "lives" in our industry, the employees. It's important that we realize that those numbers actually represent real lives and, if those employees are not happy with the benefits that their employer is providing, that certainly could affect your success with that client sooner or later.

Thus, an emailed monthly newsletter to all your clients' employees from your firm is certainly in order. In addition, I recommend taking a stack of hardcopy newsletters produced for employees and leaving them in your clients' employee lounges, cafeterias, etc. Not only will this be seen as an additional service and benefit from your clients' point of view but if done correctly, it will make a very positive impact on the employees themselves and help you really lock in that client.

Endorsements – There are many types of endorsements and I will not "endorse" one over another. Instead, I'll merely recommend you find ways to incorporate this strategy. Specifically, there are three primary types of endorsements that could be most beneficial to your firm 1) Written Endorsement, 2) Personal Endorsement and 3) Celebrity Endorsement. I'll quickly explain each...

Written Endorsement – This is more than a testimonial. In fact, this is a full letter written from one HR director (insert your key decision maker) to all of his counterparts in a given industry, printed on his company letterhead and mailed in his envelope so his counterparts actually open and read it. You pick up all the expense, of course, and your client (or you for your client) writes a recommendation letter that explains what your agency has done for his company and how you could help similar businesses.

Personal Endorsement – If your producers are getting nowhere with a prospects or group of prospects, then why not let one of your happy, satisfied clients make a personal phone call on your behalf simply letting the key decision maker know what your firm has done for them. This is what my team calls "proactive references." Instead of waiting to be asked for a reference, you go ahead and have those references talk to your potential clients. This is a powerful tactic and you'll be pleasantly surprised at how many of your clients will be more than willing to help you...if you ask.

Celebrity Endorsement – I think this concept is straightforward. Find a celebrity (minor or major depending upon your size and scope) that your target market can identify with in some way. Leverage their celebrity status to impress upon, and get attention from, members of your target market. Many firms will automatically dismiss this strategy out-of-hand because they perceive the cost will too high. In today's world though, celebrities are a dime a dozen and, therefore, often you can find a celebrity that can achieve your objectives without costing your firm a fortune.

Direct Mail – This strategy is another one that is often dismiss or overlooked. The reason being that most businesses have no idea how to properly use and leverage direct mail to get any reasonable response. They'll send out one postcard to a list, get no response, and conclude, "Direct mail doesn't work and is a waste of money." That's like asking a seven-year-old to go hit a golf ball for the first time and then, when they miss, concluding, "No one can hit a golf ball – the game is impossible."

The point is, direct mail can be a tremendous advocate for you so long as it is done correctly, and you send the right message to the right list. Almost never will a single postcard get the job done. Instead, you should be considering sending out greeting cards with personal messages to your decision makers throughout the year. Or you could implement creative 3-D mail sequences that are virtually guaranteed to grab attention.

(Find out more about what 3-D mail means in the Resources section at **www.DOorDIEthebook.com**.)

Of course there are many other prospecting and marketing tools at your disposal that you should consider but the aforementioned list will at least give you some practical insights and guidance.

EDUCATIONAL MATERIALS

In today's world, a benefits agency must be seen as a knowledgeable, leading authority in its field. The days of merely transactional relationships with clients are over. Today's post-reform world demands transformational relationships with clients. This means that education has to play a major role to best position your agency as well as to develop meaningful engagement with decision makers.

Trying to sell something is the surest way to nowhere. However, educating prospects and clients alike is a powerful away not only to build necessary credibility but to also lead a decision maker to selecting you as one of their key solutions providers.

White Papers – I'm preaching to the choir regarding this one. Our industry is inundated with white papers on virtually every related subject you can imagine. Yes, I'm guilty of producing these documents as well, and have seen significant success using them as prospecting tools and to build the ever important "credibility." Consider the subjects on which you can educate your prospects and clients and then develop a plan to release a white paper every so often to further educate them, maintain your position of thought-leadership, and, of course, remind them of your firm and the solutions you can provide.

Articles – Articles can be used much more frequently and on much smaller subjects than white papers, thus making them very useful tools to gain attention quickly on a topical issue within your marketplace. Find meaningful places to publish articles, whether in an industry publication that your target market reads and/or on a website where your ideal prospects and clients visit. Of course, you can send copies of your articles to your prospects and clients to consistently to remain top-of-mind.

Webinars – Our 2.0 world has embraced webinars with reckless abandon. That is certainly not a bad thing but it is too often the case that a webinar host will spend the entire time talking about his firm or products and services without providing any real, meaningful value to the viewer. There's certainly a time for selling but your webinar must provide content and education that your market WANTS. Ask yourself what are the five biggest challenges my target market faces that I can help them overcome, then develop a webinar for each challenge, what the solution is generally, and only then, how your firm helps its clients overcome that given challenge.

Online Video – Similar to webinars with the exception of generally more limited time. Here's a comparison that should make this more clear: white papers are to articles as webinars are to online videos. Online videos can cover one small subject, one small idea or strategy that your market needs/wants to know. On your website or a sister site, I would encourage you to develop an inventory of such videos that your clients and prospects can refer to when they have questions about solving their most pressing problems.

Ultimately, it comes down to this profound equation...

Influence = Credibility + Persuasion

Educational materials as I've described here give you both the opportunity to develop credibility and the platform from which to persuade, thus providing you with influence over prospects and clients.

Events

Hosting events provides a tremendous opportunity for a benefits firm. As you well know, successful business in the benefits world is generated by developing the best, most meaningful relationships. Events allow you not only to provide real value by educating your clients (HR directors, CFOs, CEOs, owners, etc.) but also to have personal interaction between you, your team and those key decision makers.

Let's look at three types of events you could host...

Educational Programs – Whether you decide to host your own presentations or go speak to qualified groups, finding a way to use this media and format is certainly worth the effort. There are three simple steps you should follow to make sure these programs bring a positive return to your agency.

STEP 1 **Create Your Presentation with Your Audience In Mind** – You must have something valuable and interesting to say. Without something to compelling to say, this strategy will be a waste of your time. Choose a topic that will resonate with your target market and then craft your presentation around their most pressing challenge that you can solve.

STEP 2 **Decide Where The Audience Will Come From** – You must determine if you will host an educational program or if you will simply identify qualified groups to present to. Both have their obvious advantages and disadvantages and perhaps you should test both to determine which produces the best results. If you're uncertain about this strategy in general, I'd recommend simply having one of your best producers or agency leaders speak to local civic clubs and chambers of commerce. This will give you a feel for the power of educational programs without the firm committing to hosting one.

STEP 3 **Maximize the Opportunity** – The final step is actually the most important. It's not too difficult to find an audience or to create one with clients and potential clients. But you don't want to deliver the presentation without some specific plans and goals. Decide what you want the outcome of the event to be, and then design your presentation to fulfill that goal making sure you are moving the most qualified prospects into the next step of your sales process.

Partner Presentations – Essentially, this is the same concept as above except that you will partner with a strategic business partner to host these events.

For instance, let's assume you developed a strategic referral relationship with a local accounting firm that serves your ideal prospects. (See "Strategic Referral Group" below.) You might work with them to invite their clients as their guests to attend one of your educational events. In return, you could then invite your clients to attend a session that the accounting firm would host.

Client Appreciation Receptions – I suspect this one is relatively obvious but let me offer some insights that will let you get much more out of these kinds of events than just goodwill. First, a client appreciation event can include elements of education within it, thus allowing you to probe those clients for future opportunities. Second, always invite key prospects to client appreciation events as your guests. This way, they'll get to meet and talk with current, happy clients the entire time. Finally, encourage your clients to bring guests of their own. This does build goodwill but they also will be bringing potential clients, as well.

I hope these ideas get your mind flowing on just how valuable live events can be for your firm. Beyond hosting events, you and your agency's other leaders should also accept the role of sharing information in your marketplace through public speaking. Civic groups, chambers of commerce, business groups, etc. are all optimal sites for your team to speak or at least attend to deliver worthwhile knowledge and meet potential clients.

All in all, it's easy to dismiss events due to their complex nature and having "too many moving parts," as we've heard from more than one agency leader. But that is precisely what makes them a strategy worth pursuing, as you will elevate your firm above your competition.

GROUPS

Developing groups that will ultimately support your agency's growth is a very powerful strategy in that it leverages the relationships and resources of other influential people in your marketplace.

Similar to events, groups are very engaging and allow you and your other team members to develop personal and meaningful face-to-face relationships. Beyond relationships, you can create in your clients a sense of ownership in your agency, as well as accountability and loyalty to your agency.

Let me explain a couple of ways this strategy can be manifested...

Strategic Referral Group - You are probably familiar with the strategy of having your colleagues and professional peers (who serve the same target market you do but are non-competing) refer their clients to you and vice-versa. Not only is this a very smart strategy but it can become a very effective and lucrative source for high-quality prospects. The key to this is in maximizing the opportunity. To do so, it's critical that you engage this group of influencers personally on a consistent basis. Host a dinner or meeting and invite them all. Deliver a short presentation and spend some time talking with them about your firm's goals and how they can help. Then, throughout the year, stay in touch with them, send them gifts, and meaningfully help them when you can. In other words, this should not be some abstract group but rather a group that members know they belong to and are recognized for their active participation, as in the case study below.

CASE STUDY

Strategic Referral Group

A very progressive and successful agency in Austin uses this strategy brilliantly. While it's a more involved process, the results are all but guaranteed; relying largely on this prospecting strategy, the agency has been doubling its revenues annually for the past three years.

Here's how it works. Potential referral partners (e.g., CPA, attorney, owner of a technology company with a large and quality client list, P&C agency principal) are screened by the agency for personal and professional integrity and quality of service. Once vetted, the potential partners are invited to join a small and exclusive referral group – six to eight members – which requires an annual fee of several thousand dollars. The purpose of the fee is to make the commitment to the group real and have each partner with skin in the game. (The fees are used to pay for group meals and events.)

Once the group has formed, each member is asked to determine the minimum amount of new business he needs that year from each of the other partners. Every partner then reviews the quotas that are expected of him and negotiates as necessary with partners whose quota is out of line with his quota for them. Once everyone is satisfied, each partner commits to referring enough business to the others to meet his quotas. Regular meetings are used to monitor and track progress and discuss strategies necessary for each partner to meet his quotas.

A lot of work, you say? Well, keep in mind that the agency's quota from just one partner might be $150,000 revenue from new business that year. Multiply that by the six or eight members and you've added somewhere in the vicinity of $1 million in revenue.

Using this strategy, the Austin agency doubled its revenues annually for each of its first three years in business.

Advisory Council – This brilliant concept involves creating a group made up of your best clients. These clients constitute your advisory council, which can give you important insights, answer questions, and offer enlightening feedback on your firm. Beyond that, these clients also are encouraged to become advocates and ambassadors for you firm in the marketplace, giving you referrals and endorsements to prospects.

No doubt you can think other kinds of groups that could be developed to support your agency and help it grow. It's important to note that both of the two specific groups I mentioned here have been employed by other benefits agencies with impressive results.

SOCIAL MEDIA

In today's world, no chapter on marketing would be complete without at least touching on some key strategies utilizing social media. As you know, the universe of social media changes almost daily and, ultimately, that universe is very young and relatively immature. In other words, even top marketing firms are still trying to understand and figure out the best ways to use these unique and powerful platforms.

Generally speaking, social media is exactly that; it's used for social interaction. Thus, while business-to-consumer companies have started finding effective methods to create meaningful relationships with their prospects and current clients, it's a much more complex and difficult task for a business-to-business company to socially interact in any media, much less online.

With all that said, I will give you some guidance and direction with four of the largest and most significant social media platforms. The methods I'll detail should be tested for effectiveness as you roll them out to your target market. And ultimately, if you decide to actively pursue social media as a primary marketing method for your firm, I would recommend finding a trusted social media marketing firm that specializes in helping business-to-business companies achieve success.

Facebook – Currently, Facebook is the largest social media website online and it looks like it will maintain that position for quite some time. While that does mean potential opportunity, it also means it's even more difficult to find and compel your target market members to interact with your business profile. I would highly recommend you use your firm's Facebook profile as an hub of industry information rather than only focusing on your firm. Ideally, you want to create a community of the members of your target market(s) with your firm leading the conversation. Keep the conversation delivered through Facebook casual, fun, and most importantly, engaging. The more your fans and followers engage with your firm online, the more likely that you will be front of mind when they need your services.

Twitter – Let's assume that your target market is made up of HR professionals in the financial industry. Encouraging them to follow you on Twitter can become a very useful activity for your firm in that you can now send them a quick message to their cell phones anytime you want. You might send an HR Tip of the Day or funny employee stories that other prospects or clients have shared with you via Twitter. Again, the idea is to engage and interact with your target market as well as your current clients.

YouTube – The previous category Educational Materials included online videos. YouTube can be a tremendous ally for your firm to easily and consistently deliver valuable and compelling information to your prospects and clients. The goal should not be to get a zillion views but rather to put quality information out there to the members of your targeted market to position yourself as the preeminent choice for the benefits and solutions you provide.

LinkedIn – Perhaps the best candidate for successful business-to-business marketing via social media is LinkedIn. LinkedIn has become the place for professionals to network and communicate professionally with each other. In many ways, this platform is not "social" media but rather "business" media that uses social media technology. Regardless, maintaining an accurate and up-to-date LinkedIn profile, searching out members of your target market, communicating with them, perhaps even creating a LinkedIn group, and then keeping your contacts updated can produce real, tangible results for your benefits practice. Take time each week to ensure you've made at least a few new connections and reached out to prospects and, of course, your clients as well.

Again, social media is still very much a work-in-progress when it comes to business-to-business marketing. Therefore, while you should not ignore it, you should be very careful and intentional with your social media activities. And as I mentioned previously, if you want to actively pursue social media as a preferred marketing strategy, I would recommend not doing it yourself but rather seeking out a firm that has proven results.

COMPLIMENTARY SERVICES

At last we've come to the final category. This concept of delivering free service to clients and prospects can be a game-changer for a benefits agency. Obviously, the power of such an offer is clear but the real value in these strategies comes in the form of gaining access and building a client-like relationship with a prospect. Using this strategy with current clients is just as effective because you not only provide above-and-beyond service but you also are able to identify new opportunities to help them.

I've provided just four such possible services below with explanations but I know there are certainly others that have significant value and can be delivered relatively inexpensively.

Benefits Assessment – Simply put, this is an examination and analysis of a given prospect's current situation around their employee benefits. Conduct this process as you would if the prospect had decided to become your client and had asked you to first complete such a service. I'm not going to walk you through a bunch of detailed processes here but I will say that your objective with providing this complimentary service should be two-fold 1) give the prospect an accurate report of their benefits situation this year and in the near future and 2) set-up the opportunity to go back to the prospect to explain how your firm could improve their situation.

Employee Risk Assessment –This service centers around the prospect's employees and their personal financial risks. For a prospect with hundreds of employees, it's impractical for you to conduct a risk assessment for each one unless you automate the process online. However, you could at least choose a small sample size to provide personal risk assessments to give the employees an idea of what other benefits they might need as well as to give your potential client an indication of gaps in their employees' coverage that your firm can help fill. This process can also be conducted at the HR level by conducting an assessment with HR of the risks facing employees and the availability in the benefits plan of products and services to help employees manage the risks.

Compliance Review – Like it or not, with PPACA compliance will become an even bigger issue than it has been for benefit plan sponsors. Any expert guidance you could provide to a client or prospective client would most likely be welcomed with open arms. Offering a compliance review could be a seamless way for you not only to get your foot in the door but also to discover new opportunities for you and that business to work together. (See the section on compliance services in Chapter 5.)

Health Reform Updates – Related to the compliance review but a little less technical is the idea of formerly and consistently providing important updates to your clients and prospects on developments and administrative rulings on health reform that may have an impact on them. This could be as simple as sending out a monthly email and/or hosting a quarterly event where these updates are explained. Naturally, as these issues are discussed, your firm should also weave in the solutions that you provide.

Whether you decide to add any of the services above to your arsenal of prospecting strategies or develop other kinds of complimentary services, I strongly recommend giving this strategy a try.

I've just gone over twenty different methods and strategies for you to choose from to grow your benefits agency in the post reform world and I didn't even scratch the surface of what's possible with your marketing efforts. All this to say, if you thought the post reform world could keep you from growing your business, think again.

Your agency's ability to grow, and ultimately thrive, in the face of healthcare reform is based on your and your team's vision and desire to creatively and effectively deploy these and other marketing strategies to engage both your current and potential clients.

Section FOUR

21st Century Selling
Creating a Consultative Agency

Successful people ask better
questions, and as a result,
they get better answers.
　—Tony Robbins

With PPACA already creating seismic shifts in both the broker role and broker compensation, brokers and consultants are beginning to recognize the need to become more consultative, as indicated by the almost 60 percent in the MetLife study who plan to expand their consultative services.

Becoming consultative is the key to agency success post reform. In fact, consultative selling is the foundation of the 21st Century Agency.

Consult or die

The problem is, consultative selling is a dramatically new concept for the vast majority of benefit brokers. A small number of progressive agencies – and the big houses – have been using a consultative approach for years. But most brokers and consultants haven't needed to be consultative in order to stay in business. However, those days are over.

In academe, professors live by the axiom "publish or die." In the post-reform benefits economy, brokers must "*consult* or die," their practice slowly (or perhaps not so slowly) dying of client attrition if they don't become consultative.

In this section, you'll discover the power of Advisory Selling, our proprietary consultative selling system that allows you to make sales by helping your prospects solve problems and that positions you as the client's "trusted advisor." This is consultative selling re-engineered for sales professionals in the insurance industry.

In the following chapters, I'll discuss the role of the consultative advisor and how that differs from the transactional sales style that our industry has encouraged in the past. You'll learn the secret of the Sales Triangle that I discovered one night 30 years ago in a smoky bar in Amsterdam. I'll share with you why your value as a salesperson isn't in what you sell but how you sell it and the key question that can almost by itself convert a producer into a consultative advisor.

Finally, once you understand the conceptual foundation of Advisory Selling, I'll reveal the four steps to implementing this consultative process in your own selling. This step-by-step process can move any producer from transactional selling to a consultative style that will open more accounts, sell more product, and create stronger advisor/client relationships.

You don't close a sale, you open
a relationship if you want to build
a long-term, successful enterprise.
—Patricia Fripp

12

From Transactional to Consultative Selling

For decades, insurance sales have been based on a product-centric model. Driven by carriers, whose sole purpose is to sell products, insurance sales expertise has been defined largely by product knowledge. Broker product training teaches "features and benefits." Sales training, when provided, generally is characterized by old-school techniques like overcoming objections, trial closes and "ABC": "Always Be Closing."

This antiquated sales model places the emphasis and focus on the products and, more to the point, on the need of the salesperson to close a sale. Is it any wonder that clients and prospects find most salespeople and "selling" to be, at best, a necessary evil?

But, frankly, very little selling goes on in our industry. This might be a surprise to the insurance sales professionals, many of whom earn a handsome living. These salespeople are closing sales. What I mean to say is, what most of them are doing isn't *selling*. Let me explain.

From the beginnings of the benefits industry, benefits agencies have been asked to assist employers primarily with shopping and spreadsheeting quotes on the company's health plan and, occasionally, with benefit plan design. For decades, that was all that the marketplace asked of most benefits brokers, along with providing support with billing and claims issues. Brokers were paid a sizable commission by the medical carriers for selling and servicing their accounts. Most of the selling that has taken place in our industry has involved selling a business owner on offering employer-sponsored group medical insurance.

Human quote engine

Eventually, though, at some point in time most employers were now offering group health plans, so the client already had the product...group medical. The job of brokers became primarily helping the client get the best price on a product he already had. This isn't selling; this is a transactional activity and what I call being a "human quote engine,", which is, in fact, today a service that a computer could accomplish more quickly and efficiently.

The reality for far too many producers in our industry is that *they never have had to sell*, the job simply didn't require it. (As indicated by their name, consultants in our industry often have provided a higher level of advice and guidance but when it comes to the medical, they've not been selling, either.) Prospect, approach, build relationships, follow up...yes, of course, they did that. But, for most brokers, until now the art of selling just hasn't been needed in our industry.

Selling isn't persuading

Furthermore, the most common understanding of "selling" is itself misguided, similar to the description found in Wikipedia:

Selling is considered by many to be a sort of *persuading* "art." (emphasis added)

This flows from the mistaken idea that the salesperson's job is to get the prospect to buy. As we'll see in a later chapter, that is a terribly distorted view that makes selling unproductive...and difficult.

In reality, as we've just seen, for most producers what passes for selling in the benefits industry has been transactional, at best. But transactional selling is no longer sufficient when the broker's focus is having to shift from just getting the BOR on the medical to cross-selling other products and services to help replace lost medical commissions.

No cross-selling

I know for a fact that most producers in our industry don't sell...and I'll go so far as to say they really don't know how to sell.

I know this because for the past four years or so I've been conducting our Broker Boot Camp® workshops on cross-selling voluntary for thousands of brokers across the country. Sponsored both by carriers and privately by progressive agencies for their own producers, these workshops help brokers overcome their objections to voluntary benefits and shows them how to cross-sell voluntary the right way using a consultative approach. My point here is that the reason carriers and agencies are paying large fees for these bootcamps is that producers won't – I'll say can't – sell voluntary benefits, which requires actually selling the client on the idea of offering voluntary.

NOTE: Cross-selling voluntary to HR is not a difficult sale and you'll find a primer on exactly how to do it in the Appendix.

Most producers are good at relationships and can spreadsheet to beat the band. But that's not selling. And in candid conversations I've had with many producers, they have revealed the appalling lack of sales skills or even knowledge. Again, no shame here. The skill rarely has been called for until now and how would they have learned? The carriers have long ago abolished their sales training programs after they moved away from the agent system to agency distribution. And very few agencies provide meaningful sales training and most offer none at all.

With the continuing decline in broker and agency compensation on the medical, this sad state of affairs cannot continue.

CASE STUDY

The Power of Consultative Selling

Years ago, while working for a benefits enrollment firm, I managed to get a coveted appointment with the SVP for voluntary benefits at a major regional brokerage in Ohio. He started the meeting with an invitation to pitch: "We already work with several enrollment firms. Why should we work with you?"

He was giving me the opportunity to *persuade* him that he should use our services.

But instead of a lengthy presentation about our capabilities and track record enrolling voluntary benefits, I responded with just a three-sentence value proposition on our services and then boldly stated, "But that's not what I'm here to talk with you about."

That got his attention. "What, then?" he asked.

I asked him about his firm's cross-selling efforts. After some hedging, he acknowledged difficulty getting their producers to actually cross-sell voluntary benefits. Several questions later, he confirmed they were missing their voluntary sales targets.

I then said, "What if I work with your producers to overcome their objections and train them to cross-sell voluntary? I'll even go on calls with them to help close the case. Once they're writing voluntary business, I'll enroll the cases for you. Are you interested?"

He immediately responded, "When can you come in and do some lunch-and-learns?"

BOOM!

My point? My prospect didn't need my enrollment services. What he needed was increased top-line revenue and bottom-line profit from more sales of voluntary benefits. Once I stopped trying to sell my enrollment services and started using consultative selling to show agencies how I could help them sell more voluntary benefits – producing more profits – I became top producer at my firm.

This illustrates the secret to – and the power of – consultative selling, which I teach producers through our proprietary Advisory Selling system, covered later in a coming chapter.

Critical transformation

Becoming more consultative is, in fact, the most critical area for your agency transformation to both survive the coming shake-out and emerge to dominate your market. Consultative selling is a hallmark of the 21st Century Agency because so much else flows from the added value that consultative selling brings the client:

> ➤ Differentiation from competitors;
> ➤ Justification for a service fee;
> ➤ Cross-selling of other products and services;
> ➤ Strengthened broker/client relationship;
> ➤ Increased client retention; and
> ➤ Multiple revenue streams to replace lost medical commissions.

The other transformation areas – Portfolio, Marketing and Management – exist largely to support the agency's consultative selling efforts. A 21st Century Portfolio provides the tools a consultative broker needs to solve client problems and generate additional revenue streams. 21st Century Marketing supports the consultative agency by promoting to prospects the agency's value proposition as a problem solver and communicating to clients the tremendous added value that the agency brings to the client. 21st Century Management supports the consultative agency by demanding high performance, productivity and return-on-investment (ROI) from both the agency's producers and its operations.

By moving from transactional to consultative selling, producers are prepared for success in the post-reform world.

"Gatekeeper of Resources"

There's one final, very important role that the consultative advisor plays. As I wrote earlier, the 21st Century Portfolio gives the consultative broker the tools required to solve a wide range of client problems. As an advisor with access to this well-stocked toolbox, you are acting as the "Gatekeeper of Resources" for your clients. Also known as the tollbooth position, this is an unusually powerful spot to occupy. What makes the tollbooth position so powerful? You control access to something the client wants, in this case a solution to a pressing problem. To get access, the client must pay you, as the tollbooth attendant. See how being in this position strengthens your case with the client when you move to a fee-based compensation model?

But it's about more than just money and power. There's more, you ask? Yes. You become for the HR client what I refer to as "the candy man," with the wonderful ability to give out valuable solutions to heretofore insoluble problems that had plagued the client. And if you're using voluntary benefits as the solution or the funding mechanism for the solution, then you're giving the client a solution that is free to her. What a great position to be in. You can become quite popular with your clients.

And since most brokers continue to rely entirely on their portfolio of health insurance and limited ancillary products, as a consultative advisor and gatekeeper of valuable resources you have an insurmountable advantage over almost all of your competition.

When supported by a diverse portfolio of solutions, consultative selling is the very foundation and the key value proposition of the 21st Century Agency.

You have to learn what are the prospect's problems, what is causing him pain, what is causing sleepless nights. This is what the relationship is all about. It's about how you as a salesman can help the prospect solve important problems.

—Petric (last name unknown)

13

The Sales Triangle

A simple triangle sketched on a soiled napkin changed my selling and changed my life.

It happened 30 years ago, in a dark, smoky café in Amsterdam. Seated at the bar, I'm quietly sipping a drink and recalling the fantastic art and architecture I had seen that day in one of Europe's most cosmopolitan cities.

I have no idea that within minutes I'll discover a secret that will turn me into a selling superstar.

I thought I knew how to sell. A top salesman at my company, they already called me their "sales superstar."

I'd had all the best sales training ... you know, "Features & Benefits," Overcoming Objections, and my favorite, "ABC" (Always Be Closing). I'd even been trained to use the Myers-Briggs personality matrix to create rapport.

But still I didn't know how to sell. Not the right way.

Not the way that makes selling easy. And even fun.

Not the kind of selling that eliminates almost all objections and, most important, rejection.

Imagine, selling without the fear of rejection. Without having to overcome an objection... because usually there isn't one.

What happened next in that Amsterdam bar changed my life.

He slid onto the barstool next to mine and ordered a popular Dutch liquor. He nodded politely and in good but heavily-accented English introduced himself as "Petric." (I never learned his last name. Sadly, at the end of a long evening of strong drink, I failed to get his business card.)

We discovered that we both were in sales and I soon learned that he was the top producer in all of Europe in some sort of industrial electronics.

It was after several drinks that Petric leaned in and asked if I wanted to know his success secret. "Yes, of course."

The Sales Triangle

He grabbed a cocktail napkin and at the top wrote the Dutch for "Sales Triangle" then drew a triangle divided by horizontal lines into three equal parts. Each section, labeled with a letter for a Dutch word, represents one of the three major activities of a sale and the relative amount of time a salesperson spends on that task.

Petric, pointing to the triangle, said this was how he used to sell, how most salespeople still sell, why selling is hard.

V is for "Relationship"

In translation, the letter in the top, smallest third of the triangle stood for the word "RELATIONSHIP." We almost always have to have some sort of relationship with our prospect in order to make a sale. Petric pointed out that the tiny tip of the triangle reflects the fact that most salespeople spend little time on creating a relationship with a prospect.

I assumed he meant the type of shallow relationship that we are taught to create to build rapport. But I was so wrong about what Petric really meant.

P is for "Product"

The middle section of the triangle was "P" for "PRODUCT." This larger portion of the triangle is our presentation of products or services, to which most salespeople devote much more time than to creating a relationship. Petric stated that this is where salespeople pitch their product, usually with no context or focus, so that we have to present all of our products and services. In fact, Petric observed, we make this part of the sale all about us: our company and history, our reputation, our products, our suppliers, our service, etc.

S is for "Close"

The letter "S" in the bottom, largest section of the triangle stood for "CLOSE," that miserable, wretched and usually futile effort salespeople have to make to get the prospect to buy something – anything – from the full array of products that have been thrown at them earlier. We have to work so hard to close the sale because the prospect doesn't want to buy...he doesn't believe he wants or needs what we're selling.

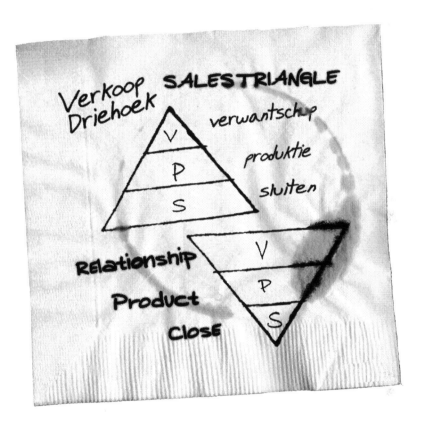

The secret of the Sales Triangle

So this was the bad news. This is what most salespeople are doing wrong to make selling difficult and stressful.

The great news was what Petric drew next on the napkin below the "Sales Triangle" ...the secret to his and my success in sales.

As he sketched it out for me on that damp napkin, I began to understand how I – and most salespeople – had been selling the exact *wrong* way.

The triangle shows the relative amount of time salespeople spend on the three phases of selling: Building the *Relationship*, Presenting the *Product* and the Making the *Close*.

It's the Relationship, stupid

After Petric drew the first, upright triangle, I could see just how counter-productive it was NOT to develop and cultivate a strong relationship with the prospect. Without that strong relationship, your only course was what one broker I know calls a "product puke," throwing up all of your products and services in the usually vain hope that the prospect will see something he'll buy. Then you have to spend even more time on the close, to persuade the poor prospect that he must buy something from you today. Ugh.

I asked Petric what techniques he used to develop rapport and learn about the prospect's family, college, hobbies, etc.

The prospect's problems

He just stared at me. "None of that's important," he scoffed. "You don't need to know any of that; you have to learn what are the prospect's problems, what is causing him pain, what is causing sleepless nights. What are his professional goals and how can you help him achieve them? This is what the relationship is all about. It's about how you as a salesman can help the prospect solve important problems."

This was novel...and extremely *powerful* information. It made perfect sense. Of course, what Petric was describing is known today as consultative selling. And 30 years ago, he gave me the keys to the kingdom.

So let's look at how selling works when done the right way.

The secret revealed

After he showed me how I and most salespeople sell, Petric sketched out another triangle but this time drew it upside down. As you can see in the illustration, the three sales phases, however, remained in the same order.

This simple inversion changed everything. Now...we spend the most time discovering and identifying the prospect's greatest needs, his biggest pain points, his career goals. Now... we know what problems to agitate to create a powerful demand for a solution. Now... we know how we can best help him solve his most painful problems.

On-point product presentation

Once we know which of the prospect's pains we can solve and we've stirred up that pain to move the prospect to a state of extreme discomfort with his current situation, now we can present the product he needs and demonstrate how it can solve his problem.

Note that you spend no less time on the product presentation than before; but now it's a laser-targeted sales pitch for a solution.

The easiest close

With the old selling style, the close was not just the most time consuming phase of the sale, it was the most painful.

Nothing is more desperate than a salesperson trying to overcome objection after objection. And the objections keep coming because the prospect simply doesn't see the need for or value in the product. But we've been trained to "Always Be Closing" and to "overcome objections."

Now that we know the prospect's pain point and can present the product as a spot-on solution, the close becomes the least time-consuming phase of the sale. *And the easiest!*

Often, the close consists of asking, "Do you want to solve your problem today?" If you've done your job well and you've also qualified the prospect as to budget, there can be no objection. The prospect has told you he needs your solution. It's not unusual for the prospect to close himself.

The Sales Triangle, as revealed to me by Petric many years ago at a smoky Amsterdam bar, helped make me a top producer. Follow the lesson of the Sales Triangle and it will drive you to the top, as well.

You can have everything in life
you want, if you will just help
other people get what they want.
   —Zig Ziglar

14

It's Not What You Sell, It's How

The Sales Triangle oriented me to sell by first building the relationship with the prospect, a relationship that is based on a sincere interest in the prospect's personal agenda, professional goals and organizational needs.

But while the Sales Triangle taught me I needed to put the prospect first and build that relationship, there were still important lessons that I had to learn about selling to become the top producer I eventually became.

These key lessons became the conceptual foundation of our Advisory Selling® system.

You Are How You Sell

You will often hear me say that the value of a sales professional isn't in *what* they sell... but *how* they sell it.

How you sell will determine how well you earn. Period.

Consultative selling is sometimes called value-added selling, because you as the salesperson are adding value for the prospect by the very sales process you use. The value you add is the value you have for the prospect.

Any fool can take an order. That's why clerks are paid a low hourly wage.

And it isn't that hard to "show up and throw up," to meet with a prospect and just present all your products with their features and benefits, pitching them against the wall and praying something sticks. These "product pitchers" will make the occasional sale but will hear "No" far more often.

I sure did. I used to give great sales presentations. Got lots of compliments and praise... "Best presentation I've ever seen" and "Thank you! What a fantastic presentation!" and even "If only I could make presentations like that." Then they wouldn't buy. Right, they would not buy what I was selling in my "fantastic" presentation. That's not good.

So it's easy to take an order and it's pretty easy to give a good product presentation. But none of that closes the sale. None of that will put serious commissions in your pocket.

Advisory selling isn't as easy as just taking an order. It requires more from you. You must become truly consultative, using questions and your knowledge of both the prospect's industry and your own toolbox of solutions to identify and solve a pain point for the prospect.

When I say pain point, I'm referring to particularly urgent and difficult-to-solve prospect needs, as distinguished from needs that are resolved easily and/or by common products.

The more urgent and difficult the need – and the extent to which you able to solve that need with a unique solution – the more valuable the solution and *you* are considered to be.

Asking what I call "discovery questions" (more about them in the next chapter) help you discover the prospect's pain points.

These are usually open-ended questions designed to elicit valuable information that allows you to uncover the prospect's real needs and emotional motivation. Equally important, they also tell the prospect that you are not just out to make a quick sale and pocket some fast cash; you're truly interested in him and his situation. What a differentiator.

When the prospect realizes that you are interested in him and not just your own agenda, he becomes more open and engaged because he is beginning to trust you...the first step to becoming his *trusted* advisor.

The more you sow, the more you reap

While consultative selling does require you to do and think more, the rewards are much greater than the traditional transactional style of selling. First, your close ratio will increase. Second, your cross-selling will improve dramatically since cross-selling basically is consultative selling, as you find additional pain points to solve for your client. Finally, both your retention and your client referrals will increase as you build a strong relationship with your clients based on trust.

If you want to be seen as the trusted advisor, you must first begin to view yourself in that way. The easiest way to do that is to begin to make the selling process *entirely* about the prospect...leave your agenda at home.

Take care of the prospect's needs and your needs will be taken care of automatically. But exactly how are you supposed to know what those all-important client needs are?

What's in it for HR?

Back when I was in production, a simple sign was hanging by my desk that read "What's In It For HR?"

A savvy sales manager had once advised me always to answer my own question, "What's in it for HR?" before presenting a new benefit to HR prospects.

Asking this question helps make the sale about the prospect, not about our own agenda and needs.

The question embodies the necessary shift in mindset from one of self-serving to serving the client's needs, from "How can I close this sale?" to "How can I help my client?" and "How can I solve my client's problem?"

This simple, albeit radical, change in mindset begins immediately to both transform the broker's role and empower him to take control of the broker/client relationship.

Advisory Selling positions the broker to be that rare sales professional that helps others get what they want. The rewards will follow as surely as day follows night.

As Zig puts it, "You can have everything in life you want, if you will just help enough other people get what they want."

But that does demand that you know what other people – your prospects, anyway – want. And there is one thing that most people in business want.

Sell profit not product

While it's sometimes called "solution selling," consultative selling is actually about selling the *outcome*, the result the client gets from buying your solution. According to Mack Hanan, who forty years ago wrote the seminal book *Consultative Selling* (still definitely worth your time), that outcome you are selling usually should be *more profit* for the client, an enhanced bottom line.

In other words, in consultative selling you don't show the prospect how they can help *you* make more money, you show the prospect how you can help *him* make more money.

You work backwards, drawing a direct line from their profit to your product or service solution that will help them realize that profit.

As a consultant, you apply tools and techniques – usually your products and services – to resolve process problems to improve your prospect's profits.

People usually are quite happy to pay a couple of dollars to make $10 or $100. That's how fee-based salespeople earn their fees. And there definitely is a lesson here for you as you consider how to transition to a fee-for-service business model.

NOTE: When you're talking to the CEO or CFO, more profit is always in demand, or, as I like to say, "Ultimately, the bottom line is always the bottom line." (This is why your goal always should be to get in front of the C-level executives. See Chapter 5 for some strategies.) But when dealing with HR professionals, you know that profit is not always their ultimate goal. So just keep that in mind. Their desired outcome very possibly involves something other than profit.

Now that you understand the core concepts behind the system, you're ready for the four-step process for implementing Advisory Selling.

CASE STUDY

Don't Show Up & Throw Up

Several years ago, I met with a carrier's top sales management executives who were interested in my providing cross-sell training at a retreat for their top producers.

After introducing me as the industry's top authority on cross-selling, my carrier contact invited me to tell the sales execs what I teach brokers.

Talk about being teed up! I had been handed a gilt-edged invitation to give my pitch to these decision makers. How quickly would you jump right into your presentation?

Earlier in my sales career, I would have leaped at the chance, spewing my sales pitch all over these execs.......and hoping that my pitch provided the solution they were looking for.

Today, however, I know better. Over the years I learned the hard way not just to "show up and throw up." (Even though it still can be tempting!)

It's so easy – and expected – for you to just walk in the meeting and go right into your presentation. But then you miss the opportunity to close a much higher percentage of your prospects.

While your prospect may expect you to launch into a product presentation, you first need to understand the real reasons and underlying motives for their interest in your product.

So I learned to focus my attention on the prospect and first ask strategic discovery questions to find out why the prospect is interested in my product and what are their goals, objectives and needs.

By asking these questions and listening carefully to the answers, I'm able to identify what benefits the product will have for them.

The prospect's real reason for wanting your product often is not the reason they think they want it. For instance, HR's interest in having you quote their medical may not be about the premium cost. The prospect actually may be frustrated with the current broker's inattention to the account or perhaps dissatisfied with some poor customer service on a billing issue. If you assume her driver is price on the medical, your presentation will miss the mark and lose you a real chance at the BOR.

So don't just show up and throw up.

Ask those open-ended discovery questions and learn what problem or pain your prospect really wants you to solve.

In my meeting with the executives, I told the group that, to be sure I could help them, I first needed to get some information from them.

I then asked each of the three execs in turn what were his goals for the event and what change did he want to see in their top producers. I carefully listened and took notes.

Now I knew the prospect's pain points, the pressing reasons why they were considering investing in my cross-sell training for their brokers.

Instead of blindly pitching my wares, I was able to craft a presentation that responded to the prospect's specific goals and objectives. In fact, I basically just fed back to them as the results of my deliverable exactly what they had just told me they wanted!

By linking my input (cross-sell training) to their desired output (brokers motivated and equipped to cross-sell more of the carrier's products), I was able to engage the executives in a valuable give and take as the executives did their due diligence on my cross-selling system.

Oh, and how did I do with the carrier I was meeting with? I was able to close the deal later that day on a follow up phone call!

BOOM!

The real problem is usually two or three questions deep. If you want to go after someone's problem, be aware that most people aren't going to reveal what the real problem is after the first question.

—Jim Rohn

15

The Four Steps to Advisory Selling

Both the MetLife survey results referenced earlier and my conversations with hundreds of brokers across the country tell me that they know they need to become more consultative in their selling. Actually doing it is another thing entirely. You and your producers likely agree.

So here are the four steps to Advisory Selling®, our proprietary training on consultative selling we provide our private consulting clients:

1) **Enter the HR conversation** – Learn about the issues – besides insurance – that concern HR. Build stronger rapport with your client with an enhanced knowledge of HR issues;

2) **Discover the prospect's pain points** – Identify HR's most pressing and vexing problems;

3) **Agitate the prospect's pain** – Create a demand for a solution by helping the prospect really understand the severity of the problem; and

4) **Offer the solution** — Show the prospect how to solve the problem and eliminate the pain.

The Advisory Selling process is designed to meet the requirements of the Sales Triangle while making it easy for a broker to begin executing the key elements of consultative selling.

We'll look at each of the four steps in a moment but first let me make an important observation. The broker accomplishes each of these steps using questions. Brokers often ask me why questions are so essential to the consultative selling process.

The power of questions

Here's the most compelling reason every sales professional should be selling with questions:

The person who asks the questions is in control of the sale.

In any conversation, someone is in charge. In a sales discussion, that person better be the broker...if he wants to close the sale. But here's where it gets somewhat counter-intuitive:

If the broker is doing all the talking, he is NOT in control of the sale.

Most of us in sales are good talkers... and that can be our undoing. The Greek philosopher Epictetus wrote, "We have two ears and one mouth so we may listen more and talk the less." I recommend *at least* that two-to-one ratio.

Here's why that's so essential to selling well, which gets us to another important reason to ask questions:

People like to buy from people they like.

But this raises another seeming contradiction: We want our prospects to like us but if a prospect likes us it is NOT because of who *we* are or what *we* know or what *we've* done or how much *we* have in common with the prospect. Prospects like us most... *when we are interested in them.*

Prospects don't want to know about us – not at first, anyway – except that we are interested in *them*.

Making a sale is not about us, it's about the *prospect.* So brokers must get to know the prospect.

The most effective way to do that is to ask questions about his business. (The smart broker already has done his research on their industry and company.) Questions are how the broker gets the prospect both to talk and to tell him what he needs to know.

Brokers should plan and write out a list of strategic questions to develop greater rapport with their prospects and to better understand them, their goals, and their challenges. (See the Appendix for a list of 31 Advisory Selling Power Questions.)

Be genuine

A word of caution. People are incredibly intuitive and can sense genuine interest – or lack thereof – so don't fake it. The broker's sincere interest in getting to know more about the prospect will be a decisive factor in building a solid client relationship.

Permission question

Before a broker starts probing for pain points, he should use some variant of this question to get permission from the prospect to ask these sometimes-intrusive questions:

In order for me to answer all your questions and learn more about you and your business, I need to ask you some questions. Is that OK?

Refer back to the prospect's giving their OK if they balk at one of your questions. Remind the prospect that the more you know about them and their business, the better you can help them.

Again, be genuine

To be effective, the broker must honor and validate what prospects think, feel and believe regardless of his own beliefs and agenda. Again, he should ask questions out of genuine curiosity and concern as opposed to asking out of self-interest. *This is what builds rapport and trust.*

It's important for the broker to remember the way selling works: He helps the prospect solve a problem, he makes a sale.

The prospect's ego and self-preservation instinct will not admit to its own pain while it senses there is a threat or it has something to lose.

It is human nature that prospects will not resist their own ideas, so the broker ultimately is helping them help themselves. This is very liberating for the prospect because the broker is providing a safe environment for him to come to his own independent conclusions.

By asking thought-provoking questions, the broker helps prospects find their own guidance and help them self-discover their priorities.

Since most people store emotional pain not in their active memories but buried deep in their subconscious, Advisory Selling uses these provocative questions to encourage prospects to safely pull up their painful memories and to actively experience it.

When asking questions, most brokers stop at the surface where it is comfortable.

They accept surface pain as real, legitimate pain when it is not. What they so often find are just indications of pain or predispositions.

For your prospects, pain is a crash course in waking up and experiencing reality.

Removing the blocks to the truth is the salesperson's mandate. Ninety percent of sales is getting to the truth. "You could look at your job as being in the varnish removal business. Since prospects put a high gloss on everything, your job is to tediously remove it layer by layer to the bare wood. Nobody is who they appear and nothing is what it appears. Personal agendas of prospects frequently are deeply hidden and emotional. Listen carefully to what is being said. What the prospect denies or ignores can be very telling as to how they view the perceived emotional cost of changing," says William Brooks in *High Impact Selling: Power Strategies for Successful Selling.*

The truth the broker needs to find is pain that is actionable. Advisory Selling helps the broker find that pain.

So let's turn to the four steps of Advisory Selling that will move the benefits producer from mere salesperson to becoming the trusted advisor.

STEP 1 Enter the HR Conversation

In transitioning to the advisor role, the quickest way to build rapport with the HR prospect in this new role is for you to enter the HR conversation the she already is having.

To better understand the prospect's needs, learn more about the issues and challenges facing HR. Some of the more vexing problems reported by HR include burdensome paper enrollments, poor employee personal data, low employee morale, poor plan participation, employee retention, and ineffective benefit communication.

Of course, HR issues range far beyond insurance and benefits. Some of the more pressing concerns include recruitment, retention, HR technology, raising productivity and training/workforce development.

To become conversant in HR matters, I urge the brokers in my training and coaching program to join the Society for Human Resource Management (SHRM) and to read HR industry publications like SHRM's *HR Magazine* and any of a number of excellent online and email HR newsletters. (See Appendix for a list of resources to help brokers speak HR.)

Then, when talking with the prospect, you can speak the language of HR – not just insurance – and demonstrate a familiarity with the issues facing your prospect.

Lunch and learn

Nothing breaks the ice like breaking bread together but regardless of where the discussion takes place, the broker as advisor must begin to learn the prospect's specific issues and concerns.

Incidentally, many brokers have confided that they often find lunch with their HR client to be an awkward experience. An excellent opening gambit and ice breaker is to introduce a list of typical benefit issues with which HR departments tend to struggle. (See the box below for the list of top HR problems.)

The broker should start the dialogue by asking for the prospect's opinion of the list. Does it conform to the prospect's experience? What issues are at the top of the prospect's own list? What issues are the most troublesome?

By inviting the prospect to review a third-party list of HR issues, the broker appeals to the professionalism of the prospect, who will begin to provide his expert opinion on the validity and pertinence of the items on the list. More important, the prospect begins to identify his own real problems and areas of concern.

Top Employee Benefits Issues

(in no particular order)

- Controlling health care costs
- Tracking employee and dependent eligibility
- Employee retention & recruitment
- Benefit communications *(specifically, employees not fully understanding or appreciating their benefits)*
- Open enrollment issues *(e.g., paper applications, multiple agents, data transfer to carriers)*
- Problems with self-service, online enrollment
- Onboarding/perpetual enrollment *(new hire orientation and enrollment)*
- Answering routine employee questions
- Billing and eligibility reporting issues
- PPACA compliance
- Poor plan participation *(e.g., HSA/HRA/high-deductible plans, LTD, 401(k), FSA)*
- Wellness/employee health management

Source: International Foundation of Employee Benefit Plans

STEP 2   Discover the Prospect's Pain Points

Pretty straight forward. If a broker is going to provide a solution to increase profits, he has to know the prospect's pain point(s) – a problem that is costing profit and keeps the prospect awake at night – that the broker can solve.

In employee benefits, we pretty much know what is costing the prospect's bottom line along with related HR issues that impact ROI on the benefit spend (e.g., open enrollment, benefit communication, employee appreciation of benefits, overutilization, turnover).

Using questions along with his industry knowledge and prospect research, the broker probes and digs until he identifies a pain point that he can solve.

When the broker identifies the right pain point, he now puts the prospect in a state of mind to demand his solution.

STEP 3   Agitate the Pain

Once the broker has identified one or more pain points that lend themselves to a solution in your toolbox of resources, he uses more strategic questions to amplify the pain and help the prospect feel the pain.

The goal of this questioning is to put the prospect in a frame of mind highly receptive to the broker's solution.

This is the critical step, where the broker creates the demand for the solution he is going to bring the prospect. He may have found a real pain point but, let's face it, no one keeps painful memories handy; we bury them away in the dark recesses of our brain. It's the broker's duty to help the prospect face the ugly truth of their situation.

The broker uses questions to drill down into that problem and agitate the prospect's pain around it. His job is to help the prospect recall just how much they hate the painful status quo. He helps the prospect dredge up all the unpleasant memories around, let's say, open enrollment or a high renewal. (This is also where the broker gets the prospect to quantify the problem's financial cost or lost profit opportunity.)

Here are a few more questions that can agitate the pain and help the prospect recognize how badly he needs a solution:

- "How does that affect your HR workflow?"
- "How is your productivity affected by that?"
- "What more important activities does that keep you from doing?" (opportunity costs)

If the broker does his job properly with these questions – asked with persistence but also with empathy and understanding – the prospect should be almost squirming recalling their misery.

This isn't sadism. The goal is to help the prospect remember just how badly he needs a solution. You are making the prospect eager for your solution.

Plus, studies show that people buy out of emotion, not logic. The emotional pain you are stirring up is a powerful ally in moving your prospect to take action and buy.

Once the prospect is squirming, the broker takes them to the very edge of the buying decision with a powerful questioning technique called "conceptual agreement."

Get conceptual agreement

The broker simply restates the pain point and confirms that the prospect would be interested in a solution to eliminate the pain. Would solving the problem allow him to sleep better at night and improve the bottom line? If the broker has done the first two steps correctly, the prospect can answer only in the affirmative. The prospect now has agreed that there would be real value in solving this problem.

This is one of the most powerful techniques a broker can employ in his consultative selling. It's a step too many sales professionals leave out. The broker looking to improve his closing ratio won't overlook this step before serving up his solution.

STEP 4 Offer Your Solution

It doesn't get any easier than this. By now, the prospect is desperate for a solution to end their pain and has agreed that solving this problem would be highly beneficial.

The broker's question, "What if I could show you a way to eliminate your pain?" opens the door to an invitation from the client to present the solution and how it can eliminate the client's problem.

Most important, if the broker properly qualified the prospect on the front end, this approach essentially eliminates objections and rejection. How can the prospect *object* to a valid solution when he has acknowledged its value? How can the prospect *reject* the broker or his solution after he has admitted his need for it?

So the broker offers his solution. Now, however, the broker can present the product or service as a spot-on solution. As the Sales Triangle in Chapter 13 indicates, the product presentation is always a major part of the sales process. But now the presentation can be laser focused on exactly how the one solution will solve the prospect's acknowledged problem, eliminate his pain, and increase the company's profits. With such a targeted presentation, the close becomes so much easier.

Having already given his conceptual agreement, quite often the prospect will close himself.

The step-by-step Advisory Selling process is highly intentional and designed to meet the requirements of the Sales Triangle while incorporating the proven strategies of consultative selling.

Differentiate by being better

By becoming a true advisor to the client, the broker differentiates himself in the most meaningful way: by being better, not just different. Different is wearing a bow tie; better is solving the client's problems. As the gatekeeper of resources that have value to the client, the broker himself becomes a valuable resource for the client.

By entering into the client's HR conversation, he not only engages the client in a way no other insurance salesperson can, he also is able to learn about the client's real needs and problems.

By identifying the client's pain and helping the client appreciate the severity of the pain, the broker creates a selling opportunity that will help the client solve his problem and eliminate the pain.

By using Advisory Selling with his prospects, the broker's sales will increase dramatically and he will enjoy the sales process and his client relationships more than ever.

Finally, by showing the prospect how to solve him problem and end the pain, the broker sells in a way that enhances his value to the prospect by better serving the prospect's needs. By bringing his client valuable solutions, the broker become his client's "trusted advisor."

What client doesn't want to keep a broker like that?

Advisory selling is the key to success for the 21st Century Agency. Those agencies that develop a truly consultative practice will be poised to emerge a winner in their market.

Section
FIVE

21st Century Management
Managing for
Maximum Results

Efficiency is doing things right
and effectiveness is doing the
right things.
—Peter Drucker

How well is your agency managed? Is it being managed to generate maximum top-line revenue and maximum bottom-line profit?

For the money you are investing in your agency, are you demanding a high ROI from your staff and your producers?

As the leader of your agency, you must hold your team strictly accountable for a high level of productivity that will allow your agency to remain profitable in the port-reform world.

In Section Five, I'll give you step-by-step guidance on transforming your management, both for sales and overall agency management. This transformation will allow your benefits firm to take on the post-reform challenges and turn them into opportunities for success by getting more out of less.

No margin for error

As our industry becomes more competitive, margins thinner, and marketing more costly, you have less margin for error. Because more top-line revenue must be driven to the bottom line, operational inefficiencies that could be absorbed in the past are no longer acceptable.

The key to 21st Century Agency management is operational efficiency and effectiveness. As Peter Drucker puts it, the key is doing the right things and doing things right. In order to achieve true efficiency and effectiveness, you will need to open your mind and your business to new management principles.

These principles include adopting the use of new tools and technology as well embracing the ideas of delegation and outsourcing when appropriate. Only by focusing on the highest-value activities and maintaining high levels accountability across the organization will an agency leader be able to achieve that ever elusive result of doing more with less.

Doing more with less

By utilizing tools and technology, delegation, and outsourcing, you will be able to make your business both more efficient and more effective. You can deploy proven software, systems, personnel, etc., that can complete tedious or lower level tasks.

In other words, you don't want to allocate your or your producers' time to tasks and activities that can be completed better and/or faster by someone or something else. Use these resources to achieve your goals faster and easier. You'll create a business that is more efficient and more effective, creating more power for your agency in the marketplace.

Also in this section, you'll discover the specific metrics that will become the drivers of your agency. These numbers provide tremendous knowledge to an agency leader and will you to determine precisely where the agency is strong and weak as well provide insight on how to capitalize on the strengths while simultaneously shoring up the agency's weaknesses.

Too many agencies have been navigated by the intuition and guesses of their leaders but in the new post reform world, a new scientific approach built on actionable data is required if the firm wants to continue to survive and ultimately thrive.

Keep an open mind as you move through these concepts and consistently ask yourself this question, "How can I apply this concept in my agency to improve my top-line revenue and/or my bottom-line profit?"

I am confident that simply by keeping that question in mind, you'll quickly find ways to improve your agency's performance, productivity and profit and move ever closer to having a 21st Century Agency.

The more we reduce ourselves to machines in the lower things, the more force we shall set free to use in the higher.

—Anna C. Brackett

16

Agency Management Strategies
A Guide to Automation, Delegation & Outsourcing

E very insurance agency leader should have two broad goals:

1)   Increasing revenue; and

2)   Increasing agency efficiency and effectiveness.

Growing revenue increases your top line, while boosting efficiency increases ROI to boost your bottom line. Unfortunately, you will find much more information and strategies for increasing agency revenue than for increasing efficiency. But the inefficiency of most agencies is what drives down bottom-line profits and drives up time demands.

In other words, you as the agency principal have to work longer and harder... to make less money.

The new watchword

As margins tighten, agency operations must become less of a drag on the bottom line. "Productivity" is the new watchword. Your operation must become leaner and more productive. Raising your expectations of staff and implementing proven systems can be powerful first steps.

Below you will find some of the top strategies used by premier agencies across North America to increase operational efficiency and effectiveness by automating, delegating and outsourcing critical tasks and activities.

By implementing these efficiency and effectiveness strategies in your agency, you can buy yourself and your staff more time for more high-value activities and drive more revenue to your bottom line, increasing both the profitability and valuation of your agency.

AUTOMATE

Agency Management Automation

The entry level into agency management automation is a *customer relationship management (CRM) system*. There is very little doubt that you already use a CRM. Just in case, however, a CRM is an integrated information system that is used to plan, schedule and control the pre-sales and post-sales activities in an organization. CRM embraces all aspects of dealing with prospects and customers, including the sales force, marketing, back office and customer service. CRM aims to provide more effective feedback and improved integration to better gauge the return on investment (ROI) in these areas.

For more advanced automation, specialized *agency automation systems* are designed to meet the needs of insurance agencies. These systems provide a higher level of agency-specific functions, usually starting with simple functions like carrier data exchange, prospect/client database management, and email automation (i.e., autoresponders). More advanced functions include increasing employee productivity, raising CSR efficiency, and automating routine paperwork activities such as generating notices, filing, and policy history tracking.

As you can see, a robust CRM or agency automation system is virtually mandatory for a benefits agency that is looking to maintain viability and see any kind of significant growth now or in the future. Ironically, many agencies may have access to such a tool but only use a small percentage of its capability. Much like the most powerful computer in the universe, the human brain, using a small percentage of the system will get the job done but the potential for more efficiency and productivity is massive.

Thus, if you find yourself in that place with your CRM or agency automation system, get your staff trained up on the system's capabilities and then hold them accountable for not only learning the application but also implementing it fully in your agency.

Phone & Voicemail

There are numerous virtual systems as well as hardware to manage your phone... answering, routing calls and recording messages. Many of the online virtual systems are quite inexpensive yet offer sophisticated capabilities, allowing even a smaller agency to appear to be a much larger and robust organization.

Marketing & Communication

Email

Automating part of the email process will dramatically enhance efficiency. An email *autoresponder*, whether stand-alone or part of an agency automation system, is an email utility, which automatically replies to an online event with a set email reply. An everyday use of an auto responder is the 'Out of Office' reply, which you can set up when you are on holiday but in sales and marketing functions, they are usually used to send an initial sales or marketing messages in response to a prospect's inquiry or response to a sales message.

An important use of email auto responders is in marketing 'drip' campaigns that send prospects and clients a steady stream of marketing and other communications. (See Prospect & Client Follow Up below)

Phone calls

As with emails, automating the outbound calling process can increase efficiency tremendously. A telephone auto-dialer is an electronic device that can automatically dial telephone numbers. Once the call has been established, the auto dialer will announce a voice message (called a robocall) to the client. These calls can be renewal reminders, relationship contacts to keep in touch with the prospect, cross-selling messages about a product, etc.

Client Newsletter

Marketing guru Dan Kennedy calls a paper newsletter mailed monthly to your client "the most powerful marketing tool ever." Such a newsletter can build a wall around your client, create referrals, and generate cross-selling opportunities. But most agencies don't produce a client newsletter – and many that have, drop the ball – because it's hard work that has to be done every month – consistently – to achieve its goals. But a *done-for-you client newsletter* gives you all of the upside benefits with your clients while requiring almost no work on your part. Some done-for-you newsletter programs even offer complete address and mailing services to make the process almost totally turnkey and hands-off.

(I discuss using a newsletter both online and offline in detail in Chapter 11.)

CASE STUDY

No More Golden Handcuffs: Creating Your Own Lifestyle Agency

Too many benefits agency owners are prisoners of their own success.

Craig Lack, the innovative and progressive principal of ENERGI, a highly profitable benefits agency in California, realized that after four years of rapid growth – a five-fold increase in revenue with no marketing spend! – he lacked the freedom he thought owning his own business would provide. While his staff was handling the administrative workload fine, he was too much a part of the process. He was constantly putting out operational fires and answering staff questions about routine activity.

For several years, Craig had been operating with five admin staff members. After losing two larger accounts that required a high level of administrative support, he replaced those larger accounts with smaller, less demanding ones and launched an automation/efficiency drive using process standardization, systems and automation to increase efficiency but maintain a high level of quality service. This reinvention of his back office allowed him to reduce his staff from five to just two. With only two highly productive administrative staff running a highly automated back office, he now was taking a much higher percentage of his top-line revenue to his bottom line – without sacrificing his client service.

More important to Craig, his newly efficient back office ran flawlessly without him. The standardization and automation freed him up to spend much of the next 18 months traveling with his athlete son to national and international tournaments across the U.S. and Europe.

There's a powerful lesson here for any agency principal.

Prospect & Client Follow Up

Forty-eight percent of sales people *never* follow up with a prospect and only 10 percent make more than three contacts. Yet research shows that **fully 80 percent of sales are made after the fourth contact** (See the box in the next chapter.)

Email and direct mail drip contact systems allow your agency to automate this critical process to stay in touch with prospects and clients and move them through your sales funnel toward choosing to do business with you or, in the case of current clients, choosing to purchase additional products or services.

These automated contact systems can make marketing communication extremely affordable. The leading system for automating direct mail, for instance, allows you to send a customized greeting card with your personalized message for as little as $1.06 and that includes postage. That's far less than half of what you usually would pay for just a card.

(For the most up-to-date list of recommended agency technology resources, please visit **www.DOorDIEthebook.com**)

DELEGATE

Far too many agency leaders have difficulty delegating lower-value activities that prevent them from focusing on high-value activities such as tracking agency metrics, monitoring progress of the strategic plan, personal development activities such as mastermind and coaching groups, and rainmaking. Yet, these are the activities that can lead to massive agency growth and profitability.

Intentional efforts to shed lower-value responsibilities through delegation is a high-ROI activity for agency leaders, freeing them up to provide more of the rainmaking and leadership that only they can offer. Moreover, by delegating these lower-value activities to staff, you increase the value of your staff and raise their sense of ownership in the agency.

Agency leaders should undertake a ruthless and in-depth analysis of their activities, asking of each, "Is it essential that I perform this activity? Does it drive the growth of the organization?" Delegating all activities that don't pass this test will greatly improve any agency leader's effectiveness.

If you need help getting this delegation process started, try this...

Make a list of the most common activities and tasks that you and the other leaders of your firm perform on a daily and weekly basis.

Next, rank each of those activities based on much value they directly bring to the firm. In other words, note whether they high-value activities, medium-value activities or low-value activities.

Then, immediately delegate all the low-activities to your staff. And consider delegating at least some of the medium-value activities to your staff or other leaders.

Finally, with the lower level activities now of your plate, you can expand the amount of time you spend on high-value activities, which should in turn produce better results for the agency overall.

OUTSOURCE

Especially for small to medium-sized agencies with limited staff, outsourcing provides an economical way to delegate. Many agencies outsource operational functions such as payroll and accounting.

Many marketing functions also are ideal for outsourcing, such as marketing campaign strategy and design, telemarketing, your client newsletter, marketing material design, etc. Activities and functions that lend themselves to outsourcing are usually either low-value activities (e.g., janitorial work or telemarketing) or highly sophisticated tasks (e.g., accounting, IT work or marketing consulting). Regardless, outsourcing is an excellent strategy for improving the efficiency and effectiveness of agency operations.

For many high-level tasks, an excellent resource is www.elance.com, an easy-to-use online marketplace where you can find reasonably priced freelance technical and creative talent.

Go back and examine the short exercise at the end of the discussion on 'Delegation'. You can perform the same exercise related to outsourcing. Consider whether your agency's staff would become more productive by not having to complete the menial low-value tasks that could be outsourced. Similarly, if certain team members are having to learn highly sophisticated skills, and that is taking up valuable time, then having those kinds of activities outsourced is most likely a better use of time, manpower and money.

In the post-reform world, the agency that embraces these strategies of automation, delegation and outsourcing while constantly working to make itself more productive and increase operational efficiency and effectiveness can expect to receive dividends in the form of happier leaders, happier staff and substantially higher agency profits and increased agency value.

Only 5% of the population is capable of managing itself.
—Jack Kwicien

17

Sales Management
Demanding Accountability

A smaller book and leaner commissions means there's no room for error in sales, either. The leads that are generated, the prospects that are called on, the meetings that are held...all must convert at a much higher rate than ever before. And each client in the book must generate more revenue for the agency. Maximum results from producers will be key and what distinguishes the winners from the losers.

In my consulting and training work with producers across the country, I can tell you that the vast majority of them are not producing at their peak capability and certainly not at a level that will ensure your agency's success in the post-reform world.

Top sales coach Kevin Trokey identifies a serious shortcoming that I've seen in almost all benefits producers:

As I coach producers, I see one common theme that really seems to hold them back: a lack of planning and accountability.

It's a shame really, and completely unnecessary. For whatever reason, producers within agencies seem to be off limits when it comes to setting expectations and monitoring (the right) results. I always hear, "As a producer, I have the ultimate accountability because I am paid on commissions."

I get that but by the time you can measure production, it's too late. Production results (versus behavioral results) are a lagging indicator and only tell you what has (or hasn't) already happened.[15]

For the 21st Century Agency, sales results – and post-reform success – depend on successful sales management. And that means demanding accountability from producers.

Forget everything you learned about sales management from the movie *Glengarry Glen Ross.*

Let me offer some proven sales management concepts, many from my friend, Jack Kwicien, a 30-year insurance veteran who learned management as a sales manager at the old Prudential. Incidentally, Jack offers a Sales Management And Recruitment Toolkit, an excellent resource for agency principals and sales managers looking for step-by-step guidance. (You can find information on the Toolkit at **www.DOorDIEthebook.com.**)

First, Jack reminds us that only 5 percent of people are capable of managing themselves. That paltry number includes your producers. Five percent. The rest require management if they are to be truly successful. That and Trokey's spot-on observations above make the case for managed producer accountability.

If you don't manage it, it's not important

Accountability is not a bad word. If sales activity is not managed, producers will not believe that their activity has any real importance. The only way to emphasize the importance of effective sales activity is by managing it carefully.

Clearly monitor and track activity objectives vs. sales/revenues and metrics by salesperson. This way you can create the right formulas to measure the effectiveness of marketing, sales and sales activities. The goal is not only to track numbers but also to work with the producer on improving his results by improving his prospecting activity.

Activities, not results

Manage activities. *You cannot manage results.* Measure results but manage activity. Make sure that you and your producers understand that only activity counts...good results will follow good, consistent activity.

"Plan your work, work your plan." Cliché as it may be, this is a key axiom in sales management. Once a producer decides on a course of action for the

---

[15] "What Holds Producers Back?" Be Advised Blog. www.eba.benefitnews.com. Retrieved 08/22/2012.

week, manage him or her to work that plan. In the words of Aristotle, "We are what we repeatedly do. Excellence, then, is not an act but a habit." Ninety-five percent of producers have to be forced into the habit of consistent productive activity.

And you must hold them strictly accountable. Don't accept excuses. Your producers can make money or they can make excuses; they can't make both. In fact, the more excuses you hear, the more likely it is you're listening to a producer who needs to be fired. George Washington Carver once said, "Ninety-nine percent of all failures come from people who have a habit of making excuses." Expect results, not excuses.

Manage the important, not the urgent

Don't let "management by crisis" distract you from the importance of managing the fundamentals, the daily blocking and tackling of sales that results in prospects contacted, appointments set, follow-up done, prospects converted, sales written. This is where the sales are made.

Coaching persistence

President Calvin Coolidge once said, "Nothing in the world can take the place of persistence."

That's nowhere truer than in sales.

According to the National Sales Executive Association, eighty percent of sales are made on the fifth to twelfth contact but only 10 percent of salespeople make more than three contacts with a prospect.

Any doubt why the sale goes to the elite salesperson who persistently follows up with those prospects that don't say "Yes" on the first try?

...and that's 98 percent of them!

The following statistics should be sobering for any salesperson and, especially, for any agency leader.

Persistence, Sales & Lost Opportunity

You will be shocked by these statistics relating to sales follow up:

- 48% of salespeople never follow up with a prospect.
- 25% of salespeople make a second contact and stop.
- 12% of salespeople make three contacts and stop.
- *Only 15% of salespeople make more than 3 contacts.*

But here's the truly tragic part, where it hits you squarely in the wallet:

- 2% of sales are made on the first contact.
- 3% of sales are made on the second contact.
- 5% of sales are made on the third contact.
- 10% of sales are made on the fourth contact.
- *80% of sales are made on the fifth to twelfth contact.*

Source: National Sales Executive Association

Follow up plan

Unless your producers defy all statistics, they simply are not doing their job like they should when it comes to following up on new client opportunities.

Be sure to help your producers develop a specific follow-up system to keep in touch with the prospect and keep the prospect in play.

An effective follow-up campaign should include multiple types of contacts, including email, direct mail (thank you note, greeting card, post card, etc.), your monthly client newsletter (emailed at least, paper mailed is far better and much more effective), and phone calls.

Spread out contacts so as not to seem overly aggressive but keep up the contacts until the prospect buys or says, "Stop."

This is essentially about creating an effective sales funnel that moves prospects ever closer to becoming a client. Moreover, per the earlier discussion of automation and delegation, this funnel should be as automated as possible to free up producers to be prospecting or closing. Fortunately, there are highly efficient automated systems to reduce the work in getting most of these tasks completed. (For an up-to-date list of recommended technology resources, visit **www.DOorDIEthebook.com**)

Monday goal setting

Meet briefly with each producer on Monday morning to establish the activities and activity goals for the week. This meeting doesn't need to be any longer than five minutes. Encourage and mentor when necessary. Set the tone for the week and ensure that each producer has a plan and knows he will be held accountable for following his plan.

Friday review

Meet again with each producer on Friday to review and discuss his week's activities. Discover why goals weren't met or activities accomplished. One great idea Jack suggests is to meet with producers in descending order of production for that week, after which they are free to leave for the day. In other words, top producers are the first to have their weekly review meeting and the first to leave, in time for a leisurely lunch or that afternoon round of golf, perhaps. Meet with producers at the bottom of the production chart at the end of the day, ensuring they put in a full day's work.

An agency principal who is one of our standout clients has become rigorous in managing producer activity. He takes his approach to another level, holding:

> A Monday morning sales meeting for the entire team to set and review team sales goals and to recognize individual and team sales achievement;

> A five-minute private meeting with each producer first thing every morning to discuss his activity plan for the day; and

> A Friday afternoon private meeting with each producer to review his week's activities.

By expecting and demanding a high level of production from his producers, this agency leader has qualified for every carrier bonus, awards trip and incentive program but one over the past year. You might consider his approach.

A word of warning

Applying an effective sales management process never made a manager popular with his sales team. Producers can be over-optimistic and some can even be desperate. Either way, they don't like sales managers raining on their parade. And as Kevin Trokey noted above, benefits producers consider themselves accountable to no one but themselves. *But that should be an extremely secondary issue.* It's much more important to know the facts, be able to intervene to increase the chances of winning an account, and be able to create accurate sales forecasts. And to let a producer go when need be. If he can't or won't do the work to generate new business for your agency, do you really want someone like that around your other producers?

Tracking activity

So documenting producer activity and tracking persistence are critical in creating a high-performance sales organization. While this activity is essential to improving sales results, we've seen that the sales manager who seeks to implement this will encounter pushback from most producers. And not all managers are comfortable embracing the sometimes necessary "bad guy" role. Yet the post-reform survival and growth of the agency requires that producer activity is tracked and managed.

There is, however, an easier and automated way for sales managers to both track producer activity and identify areas for improvement.

A veteran insurance sales manager has created a simple-to-use but powerful sales management tool called OnTarget that allows a sales manager to track producer activity easily and less intrusively and measure each producer against benchmarks that ensure acceptable levels of production. Easily adaptable to each agency's specific sales protocols, the OnTarget software indicates and provides actionable evidence of those areas in which a producer needs guidance or additional sales training. We use OnTarget with our private agency clients and Agency Growth Mastermind Partners. (For more information, see OnTarget in the "Million Dollar Rolodex" at **www.DOorDIEthebook.com**.)

Incentives and voluntary benefits

One critical mistake I see agencies make with cross-selling initiatives for voluntary benefits is failing to compensate producers on the voluntary sale at the same level as the medical. Since the voluntary benefits selling process is completely different – and more complex – than the medical and ancillary sale, it's critical to provide meaningful incentives to encourage producers to step out of their comfort zone and attempt the voluntary sale. Not only is strong comp essential for a successful voluntary cross-selling program but recognition of cross-selling success will also motivate producers to cross-sell.

Reward & recognize

Because sales professionals are competitive, they will know who is atop the sales leader board and commission and bonuses are the standard reward. But Jack reminds us that salespeople respond to rewards *and* recognition... and, ultimately, recognition is a more powerful motivator. So establish a good recognition program to get the most from your sales force.

Today an agency's challenge is to do more with less, to demand more production from your sales team just as you must demand more efficiency from your office staff. Strong sales management is an essential key to success for the 21st Century Agency.

A manager is responsible for
the application and performance
of knowledge.
    —Peter Drucker

18

Keeping Score in Your Benefits Agency

There is no more vital activity an agency leader should perform than to monitor the agency's numbers and actively track results. After all, decisions made for marketing and sales should be based as much as possible on previous results and data.

As mentioned in Section Four, the key is to do more of what does work and less of what doesn't. And of course the only way to accomplish that is to know what is working and what isn't.

Here's a terrifying truth... Based on our experience, most agencies (probably around 80-90 percent) are not consistently and carefully measuring their sales and marketing results. In essence, when faced with a sales or marketing question, agencies are making critical decisions on anecdotal information, guesses and hunches. In other words, they "hope" their decision will create more commission in their pockets but in reality there is no logical basis for that result. The U.S. Army has a saying: "Hope is not a strategy."

If you happen to be one of the elite few who are almost religious about tracking your results, then hats off to you and keep doing it. This article will give you some ideas you certainly can use to make your efforts easier and more effective.

On the flip side, if you're one of the agency leaders who knows you needs to be tracking results, measuring your success and failures, and using that information to consistently improve your business, then you should read the rest of this chapter with a highlighter in hand and, then, immediately start applying the concepts that I'm about to present to you.

Agency leaders who consistently "keep score" in their business are virtually always much more successful than their counterparts who are not tracking and measuring results. This is not surprising at all when you realize that the only way to know what is making (and costing) you money is to keep track of it. And one of the simplest and fastest ways to grow your business is to do more of what is already working for you.

Beyond that, you certainly don't want to keep flushing money down the proverbial drain on an activity that isn't working at all. And the only way to know that is to track everything.

So, unless you're just doing this "benefits thing" as a hobby... or unless you have millions of dollars you can afford to just blow... or unless you want to keep struggling day after day "hoping" your next decision will be profitable, then you have no choice but to actively "keep score" in your business.

First things first, you need to know what you should actually be measuring. You need to know what aspects of your business you need to be keeping score on. Below is a list of the top ten metrics you should know and be monitoring regularly.

This may sound like a lot but, in actuality, it's not. In fact, there are many other key metrics that you will probably want to begin tracking and measuring once you've implemented tracking systems for these. Regardless, many of these metrics are related to each other. And the truth is, the information you need to determine each of these metrics is easily tracked and the math needed is easily done.

As you move through these ten metrics and their explanations, you'll notice I've listed them under three categories to make them easier to remember and understand. These categories are **Cost Metrics, Accounting Metrics** and **Value Metrics**.

Now, I'll briefly break down each specific metric for you, show you how to figure each and provide you a simple way to track each number.

Cost Metrics

Cost Metrics, appropriately so, are focused on metrics where cost is somehow measured and then reported back to the agency.

Return-on-Investments (ROI) – This is one is pretty obvious but the key is it does not refer to only one aspect of your business. You need to calculate multiple returns-on-investment numbers for your agency. For instance, you need to know the ROI for each of the following: sales activities, marketing activities and your overall agency ROI.

Here's the math for determining your ROI:

Take the amount of income you received (return) and divide that number by the expense of the activity you're measuring (investment). This will result in a new number. ROI is normally written and discussed as a ratio. So this new resultant number is related to the number 1 in ratio form. Here's a simple example for marketing ROI:

Agency XYZ spends $10,000/month on marketing efforts. He's determined that his marketing activities are responsible for $30,000 of income per month. Therefore, $30,000 divided by $10,000 equals 3. Putting this new number into the ratio, it would be 3:1. This tells us that for every $1 Agency XYZ spends on marketing, he gets $3 back.

This is of course an elementary example just to show you the process. You should not only calculate ROI on your all your marketing activities together but also calculate the ROI for each individual marketing strategy you use. And you should do the same for your sales activities and for your business a whole as well.

ROI is one of the most critical of all these ten metrics, so make sure you understand this concept and then apply it ASAP.

Cost Per Lead – Cost Per Lead is simply the cost required to generate a new lead. Therefore, this metric is very easy to determine if you only buy leads. However, most likely, you have multiple sources of leads. As such, you need to figure the amount of time and money required to generate one lead. Remember time is money so you'll need to valuate your time as you calculate this metric.

Let's look at another Agency XYZ example:

This hypothetical firm has five lead generation methods. He has associated the following costs to each one and also determined the number of leads created from each source. The chart on the next page shows how the agency (and how your agency) tracks these numbers.

Lead Generation Results

Lead Source	Cost ($) Per/Mo.	# of Leads o Generated/Mo.
Events	$1,000	100
Direct Mail	500	75
Networking	200	20
Website	50	40
Yellow Pages Ad	50	15
Total	**$1,800**	**240**

This chart allows us to instantly calculate the Cost Per Lead (Cost divided by Number of Leads) for any one of the methods used as well as to instantly determine the total average Cost Per Lead, which is $7.50 ($1,800 divided by 240 leads).

Naturally, you'll rightfully have more than just five lead generation methods to track and calculate. This knowledge will let you know, at a glance, which methods are working really well and which ones are not; thus, which ones you should invest more money into and which ones you should not. For instance, we can instantly tell that Agency XYZ's website is his most effective lead generation method. Therefore, those agency leaders should consider finding ways to drive more and more traffic to his website.

Cost Per Sale – This metric is very similar to the previous one with the exception you have to take one more step. The easiest way to do this is to simply add a fourth column to the Lead Generation Results chart we just created. That fourth column would measure Converted Leads or Sales. Let's take a look at that fourth column for Agency XYZ:

Lead Generation Results

Lead Source	Cost ($) Per/Mo.	# of Leads Generated/Mo.	# Converted (Sales)
Events	$1,000	100	20
Direct Mail	500	75	35
Networking	200	20	10
Website	50	40	10
Yellow Pages Ad	50	15	5
Total	**$1,800**	**240**	**80**

Now armed with this information, we can examine which marketing methods are truly the most effective. After all, as nice as leads are to create, what pays the bills are converted leads and actual sales.

To determine Cost Per Sale, you simply calculate Cost divided by Number of Sales. Following this through for Agency XYZ, it's easy to determine which marketing method is the most effective. After dividing each one out, you'll notice that the website is the most effective method for Agency XYZ to create new clients. The agency's Cost Per Sale from his website is only $5! Agency XYZ's total Cost Per Sale for all his methods equals $22.50.

In other words, to create a new client, it costs Agency XYZ an average of $22.50. For an average benefits agency, this is probably a very low estimate but I just wanted to keep the numbers small and simple to illustrate the concept. Hopefully, you can understand just how much these metrics empower you to make the right decisions in your business.

ACCOUNTING METRICS

By "accounting" I'm not referring to balance sheets, payables or expenses. Instead, these metrics simply refer to numbers of things. ("Counting Metrics" just didn't have the same ring to it.)

While I'll only be going through two of these Accounting Metrics, they are critical to your growth and you must consistently measure them. The good news is, once you have determined them the first time, it's just a matter of keeping them up to date, which is not a difficult task.

Number of Clients (past and present) – This is as simple as it sounds. You need to keep an up to date accounting of the number of clients you have now and had in the past. You may already have this easily available to you. One issue also to consider is that if you work in both the individual and group sides of the industry, you should segment out those clients from one another.

Why keep a list of past clients? Well, several reasons. First, at some point you managed to attract them as a client, and so it stands to reason you might be able to do so again.

Second, they know you and unless you don't want to work with them or they had a horrible experience with your firm, you still have a relationship with them that should be cultivated, not just in hopes they will return to you but also for the purpose of producing new sales opportunities and referrals.

Finally, reactivating past clients is often much less expensive than generating new clients. Thus, if you ignore those past clients, you most likely are also ignoring good opportunities as well.

The Number of Clients metric is critical to being able to accurately predict your income and monitor your growth on an ongoing basis.

The second Accounting Metric is...

Average Number of Products Per Client – Simply put, this metric is an accounting of the number of products each of your clients have bought from you on average. The purpose of this metric is to show you how well your firm is cross-selling and precisely where you have opportunities to round accounts within your current book.

The key word is "average." I realize that each of your clients has different situations and require specific kinds of solutions. Some of your clients may have five different products with you while others only have one product with you. You need to be looking for the average number of products per client.

Obviously, the higher that average is, the better job you're doing of cross-selling multiple products to your clients. In order to determine this metric, follow the simple procedure below:

1. Review your list of clients.
2. Next to each name put the number of different products that client has with you.
3. Add all those numbers together.
4. Divide by the total number of clients.

The result will be your Average Number of Products Per Client.

As you go through this process, you'll also be identifying the specific clients that are prime prospects for account rounding. Naturally, the clients that you've only sold a couple of product to are the ones to begin contacting and cross-selling.

Now that you know the Average Number of Products Per Client, you can consistently monitor that number and concentrate on your cross-selling efforts so that number increases. As this metric improves in your agency, your profits will be increasing, your retention rate will increase, and your referrals will also jump.

The higher the Average Number of Products Per Client, the more stable and more lucrative your business will be from a valuation standpoint as well. So do not underestimate this metric.

VALUE METRICS

Value Metrics are the measurements you make that are in direct proportion to the value of your agency. In other words, they're the fun ones to look at for those who are successful. And they are the depressing ones to look at for those who are struggling.

But the goal here is not to make you feel unnecessarily good or bad about where you are.

Instead, the goal is to help you understand how these measurements work and how looking at them can guide your agency to consistent growth and success.

Let's begin with...

Client Retention Rate – One of the most telling pieces of an agency's success or failure is its ability to keep current clients over the long term. In other words, how well the agency retains its clients. Your retention rate speaks volumes about your agency, how you do business, your relationships with clients, your client service, your value proposition, etc.

To calculate your Client Retention Rate, just look at the last 12 months. Create a list of all of your clients at the beginning of that 12-month period. Next, go over that list and count the number of clients from that list who are still your clients. All you do then is take the number of clients that were kept (retained) and divide that by the original total number of clients. Move the decimal two places to the right and you'll have your retention rate.

Here's a quick example:

12 months ago, Agency XYZ had 150 clients.

From that book, the agency kept 128 clients during those 12 months. (He lost 22 clients.)

$128/150 = 0.8533 => 85.3333\%$

Agency XYZ's Retention Rate = 85 percent (rounded to the nearest percent)

You might also look at the retention rate based on the number of lives you serve. This will be a critical metric as well especially for valuation purposes.

Being in the industry and business you're in, I would set your goal to have no less than a 90 percent retention rate. Or you should not be losing more than 1 out of 10 clients each year. So Agency XYZ in our example still has some work to do.

If your retention rate is lower than 90 percent, then you need to carefully reexamine your communication with your current clients and make sure you are providing compelling, educational and valuable information to your clients on a consistent basis (at least monthly).

Average Initial Transaction Size – One of the fastest and easiest ways to increase your agency's profitability is by putting some real focus on this key metric. By increasing the average initial transaction size when working with a new client, you can quickly and substantially increase the bottom line.

Determining your Average Initial Transaction Size is as easy as you imagine it to be. For your newest 10-25 clients, write down how much your profit was from the first product or set of products they bought from you.

Then, just average up those numbers by adding them all together and dividing by the number of clients you counted.

A simple brief example:

Agency XYZ recently added 12 new clients. The total of his adding up all the initial commissions from each one was $172,143.50.

Broker Bill then divides $172,143.50 by 12 to get his Average Initial Transaction Size which is $14,345.29. The agency now knows that, on average, when he gets a new client that client will initially be worth $14,345.29.

Of course over time, the firm's clients will probably buy other products and renew year after year but for this metric, we're only looking at the initial size of commission from a new client.

But BEWARE...Never sacrifice a good client trying to make a bigger sale! What I'm referring to is the understanding that a good client relationship will pay off much more over time than one quick big payday.

Naturally, the best way to increase your Average Initial Transaction Size is to cross-sell multiple products that solve client needs.

Average Client Annual Value – This is a close cousin to Average Initial Transaction Size but there is a key difference. Where the previous metric measures only one transaction, this metric measures all transactions during the whole first year.

By measuring average annual value of your clients, you can see how effectively (or not) you are cross-selling other products they probably need.

If your Average Client Annual Value is very close to or similar to your Average Initial Transaction Size, then that tells you know you're not adding multiple products to your client base. And that means both you're leaving money on the table and your clients are not getting the solutions from your agency that they most likely need.

Here's how to figure this one out...

Create a list of your clients that have been your client for the entire past 12 months. (DO NOT count clients added during the past 12 months!) Next, for each one determine how much commission they generated for you. Add all those amounts together and then divide by the number of clients in that list.

Again, let me share a quick example:

Agency XYZ makes a list and finds out it has 10 clients that have been a client for the past 12 months. For each one, the commission generated during the 12 months is added up. All those amounts are then added together, which totals $185,722.50. All that's left for her to do is divide $185,722.50 by 10.

$185,722.50 / 10 = $18,572.25 (rounded to the nearest penny)

Comparing this number to Agency XYZ's previous metric Average Initial Transaction Size, we find the following:

Average Initial Transaction Size = $14,345.29

Average Annual Client Value = $18,572.25

The difference between the two is just over $4,000. That means that Agency XYZ is increasing client commissions (on average) by that amount during the first year of working with a given client. You will have to determine what target amount is desired for your agency.

Now to the final value metric...

Total Lifetime Value of a Client – This is simply the total amount of money that an average client is worth to you for the duration that they are your client. This metric tells you much about the quality of your agency in the eyes of your clients. If your Total Lifetime Value of a Client is really high, you are doing well. If it's not, you've got room for improvement and positive changes.

To calculate this metric, look at how many clients you have and or each one, write down how many years they've been with you. If a client has been with you for 2 years and 8 months, I'd round to the nearest half year so in that case it would be 2.5 years.

I realize this may take a little time but the good news is, you don't have to calculate your Total Lifetime Value of a Client very often. In fact, I'd suggest you do so only twice each year.

Once you've got the number of years each client has been with you, you need to average those numbers. So add up all those years, and divide by the number of clients you have. This will give you the length of time a client stays with you on average.

Next, you need to know how much each client is worth to you per year. In other words, you need to know your Average Annual Client Value that was discussed earlier.

Take your Average Annual Client Value and multiply it by the Average Length of Time a Client Stays with You. That resulting number will be your Total Lifetime Client Value.

Once again, we turn to Agency XYZ for a quick example:

Agency XYZ has 134 clients (new and old) and after determining how long each client has been with his agency and then dividing by 134 (number of clients), he figures out the average length of time he keeps a client = 3.75 years.

The firm then takes the clients it's had for the entire past 12 months (not newest clients) and adds up the commissions from them for the same time period and then divides by that number of clients. Doing so, we'll assume Agency XYZ determines the Average Annual Client Value = $18,572.25.

Now when he multiplies $18,572.25 by 3.75 years to determine the Total Lifetime Value of a Client, which in this case = $69,645.94.

That means that when Agency XYZ adds a new client, on average, $69,645.94 has just added been added to the bottom line! You need to start thinking in these terms. Also, note that this number does not include all the people that may have been referred to Agency XYZ by his happy clients.

Think about how this paradigm shift in your thinking could cause you to look at you acquire and retain clients in a totally different way. Now, you know that when you add a client, you've just added a BIG number to your bottom line so long as you do what you've been doing!

The next and final metric is (drum roll please)...

Projected Annual Earnings – This is how much gross revenue you expect to bring in each year.

The best way to determine this is by taking your current number of clients and multiplying that number by your Average Annual Client Value.

Here's Agency XYZ's example:

Agency XYZ has 134 current clients and his Average Annual Client Value is $18,572.25, thus his Projected Annual Earnings are $2,488,681.50.

Agency XYZ can now predict the future so to speak by knowing ahead of time exactly what can be expected based on the current situation. Therefore, the agency leaders will know what they need to do to achieve their goals.

I encourage you to determine these metrics for your agency.

I know it's not the most fun thing to do in the world but I'll tell you this...It's a heck of a lot more fun to figure out your numbers, track them, and know exactly what action you need to take to succeed rather than throwing stuff up against the wall and seeing what sticks.

Metrics allow you to take back control of your agency, and purposefully take action. After all, as valuable as it is emotionally and mentally, hope is simply NOT a viable marketing strategy for your agency!

Section
SIX

Putting It All Together
for Your Agency
Taking Your Agency from
Base Camp to the Summit

Today is your day! Your mountain
is waiting. So... get on your way.
—Dr. Seuss

W e're at that point where I'm about done and it's just about your turn. But before you "get on your way" and start your climb to the top, let's make sure you can get there...and as fast and easy as possible.

The final three chapters are about one single goal: Getting your agency from wherever it is today up the mountain to become a 21st Century Agency.

Again, this is no easy task. I wouldn't dream of guaranteeing you a successful journey. But you do have a comprehensive map that can guide you up to the summit.

The obstacles you face are two-fold:

1) The sheer difficulty of reinventing a business model; and

2) The challenge of instituting these changes alone, without external support.

However, I'll give some best-practice strategies that can make your journey faster and easier. These are drawn from the lessons in the Prologue and are based on the British expedition and their successful journey to the top of Mt. Everest.

In the first chapter, I'll show you how to evaluate your situation with your own agency. First, we'll look at where exactly your agency is on the mountain right now, where your Base Camp is in comparison to the a 21st Century Agency at the summit.

And, second, we'll look at the resources you can marshal to support you on your journey up the mountain. The success of Edmund Hillary and the British expedition was due to several key factors that we'll revisit and explore. As much as possible, you need to create your own expeditionary team to make your journey faster and easier.

In the next chapter, we'll examine how to create a realistic timeline for your journey of reinvention. The process of reinvention will go on forever if you don't set a target date to be that 21st Century Agency you want to be. And the journey will be terribly discouraging and meandering if you don't establish well-defined milestones, your camps, as you make your climb. Reaching these camp milestones will give you reason to celebrate your achievements and an opportunity to regroup and refresh for the climb to the next Camp.

In the final chapter, I'll lay out your next steps to get started on your journey to the top of our industry in your market as a reform-proof 21st Century

Agency. And I'll reveal how you can almost guarantee you will make it to the summit and have your agency ready by 2014.

If you can implement these strategies, you will dramatically increase your odds for success, the likelihood you will stand on the summit and announce, "Well, Nelson, we knocked the bastard off."

You cannot succeed by yourself.
It's hard to find a rich hermit.
—Jim Rohn

19

Evaluate Your Current Agency Situation
Establishing Your Base Camp

Your success in this journey of reinvention, this climb up the mountain to becoming a 21st Century Agency will require a tremendous amount of energy and commitment on your part. Even then, your task will be terribly difficult if you don't give yourself and your agency every advantage to succeed.

As the hopeful but hapless Maurice Wilson made plain, climbing Everest alone, without support and guidance, is a fool's errand. And as Wilson discovered, failure can be fatal.

Wilson was terribly naïve and remarkably unaware of his true situation and circumstances. If you desire to succeed in your climb to the summit, you must be ruthlessly honest with yourself about your own situation and capacity. While Wilson blithely dismissed experienced guidance and rejected effective tools, you must take a serious inventory of your resources before you begin your journey. Your ultimate success or failure will depend on the help you can leverage during your climb.

Base Camp

As you prepare your assault on the mountain, you first need to establish your Base Camp – that is, where your agency is now compared to a 21st Century Agency. Review the four steps of reinvention in Chapter 4 and then look at your agency; have you already moved your agency up the mountain by instituting some of these strategies?

No two agencies will start this journey to the summit from the same spot. You may already have gotten a start on diversifying your portfolio or you may already be tracking your key agency metrics. You might already have trained your producers on consultative selling or you might be using sales management best practices in your agency now.

Simply note what parts of the reinvention plan you have in place now. Each of the four steps is one of the milestones, a "camp," that marks your progress up the mountain. We'll look more closely at these milestones in the next chapter. Elements of the four steps are checkpoints between the camps along the route up the mountain. Even if you haven't fully implemented one of the four steps but you do have elements of the step already in place in your agency, you're further up the mountain and closer to the top than you would be otherwise.

Wherever you are, whether you're starting at the base of the mountain, at a checkpoint further up, or at Camp I or maybe Camp II, that's where your Base Camp is. And that will determine the starting point of your journey up the mountain toward becoming a 21st Century Agency. The higher up the mountain you already are, the shorter the time and the less effort required to reach the top.

Support for your climb

Now that you know the location of your Base Camp, let's look at what else you need around you to support your climb. You already have your map but you may have other valuable resources that can increase your odds on your journey up the mountain.

You remember that the British expedition that conquered Everest was a well-funded, well-equipped group effort. The climbers in the expedition had four key advantages that allowed their success:

> ➢ A committed team, or peer support;

> ➢ Expert guidance;

> ➢ Proper tools; and

> ➢ A good map.

Let's take a look at each of these in reverse order and how you can obtain similar advantages for yourself.

A good map

Great news! Check this one off on your To Do list, since you're holding the right map in your hands. Because this is, to my knowledge, the only comprehensive and defined plan for agency reinvention available, so as the only map it's the right map. But, beyond that, these strategies and tactics you will be implementing in your agency are practical and proven.

So with a good map to guide your climb literally at hand, what about the right tools?

Proper tools

Having the right tools is about getting the job done faster and better. Hillary and his team used the most advanced climbing apparatus; specialized oxygen breathing gear, state-of –the-art clothing, sleeping bags and tents; and they were trained in the latest climbing techniques. Unlike Maurice Wilson, they understood that they needed every advantage in climbing Everest if they were to reach the summit.

For your own successful climb, you need the best tools and techniques you can get.

More good news! In addition to the proven techniques and valuable tools found in the various chapters (e.g., the Top HR Problems list in Chapter 15), Scott and I have included some other useful and powerful tools in both the Appendix and online at **www.DOorDIEthebook.com**. You can access the tools online simply by going online and registering your book.

The resources in the Appendix and online include a detailed guide to cross-selling voluntary benefits with a consultative approach (the only correct way to sell them); the Prospecting Matrix for identifying ideal prospects; a list of Advisory Selling Power Questions to make your consultative selling easier and more effective; and a USP Formula Cheat Sheet to assist you in creating your core message.

However, as good as the tools and techniques we've provided you are, there is a wide range of additional tools that you could employ to shorten your journey, make it easier, and improve your results. You can get those tools from industry experts who can guide you on your climb.

Expert guidance

Don't think that Edmund Hillary deserved most of the credit for climbing to the top of Mt. Everest; he certainly didn't think so. As part of the team, the British expedition hired 20 experienced Sherpa guides, including Hillary's climbing partner Tenzing Norgay. These expert mountaineers were extremely knowledgeable about the local terrain and helped the climbers avoid pitfalls, literally; taught them new climbing techniques; and guided them to safer routes and shortcuts that saved precious time and energy.

To increase the odds for your climb, you must identify your own expert guides from our industry who likewise can provide you with wise counsel and direct you to easier and better paths up the mountain. These would be experts in sales, marketing, agency management, and specialized areas such as sales management, referrals, online marketing, compliance, agency technology, etc.

In addition to providing you with technical expertise, a few of the experts in our industry are capable of serving as a mentor on your journey. They are highly experienced working with principals to improve agency performance and know the challenges you face as an agency leader. Regardless of your own experience and length of time in the industry, the right mentor(s) can work alongside you during your entire journey to make your task of reinventing your agency so much easier and your results so much better.

To start assembling your expert guides, find out who the industry recognizes as authorities on their subject. Look at who speaks at industry conferences, writes in industry publications, leads workshop and seminars, and already advises agency leaders like you on their areas of expertise.

Once you've identified your expert guides, you have a couple of options on how you can access them. Remember that the British expedition was well-funded and invested in a large group of expert guides. Consider their example. On the other hand, unlike the Everest expedition, you don't have to take all of your guides with you for the entire journey. The best way is to hire them as needed to guide you through part of your climb. For example, you don't need a sales management guru to help you create your marketing program, just your sales management system.

The budget approach is far less effective but still an option. Many industry experts do write frequently, some regularly. Their articles and white papers can serve as a poor man's consultant. If you can catch some of them at a conference, you might be able to squeeze an answer or two or a few bits of advice from them for free. This no-budget approach is not advisable and is a very poor substitute for actual engagement of these experts to guide you personally on your agency reinvention journey up the mountain.

Making the investment

Consider this. What are your agency's annual revenues? What is your personal income from your agency? What is it worth to you to preserve that, at the least...even likely increase that amount? There's a time-honored concept known as "buying money at a discount." Effective sales training is a good example of this; you invest $10,000 and your newly trained producers generate an additional $100,000 in new revenue that year. You just bought $90,000 for only $10,000. Wouldn't you be asking, "How often can we do this?!"

Don't ignore the lesson from the British expedition. Large, important goals deserve – and require – lots of resources. Your climb, your effort to re-invent your agency as a 21st Century Agency should be well funded. This is an investment in your future and your continued ability to earn a good living that a 21st Century Agency can ensure. Commit to the proper funding for the proper resources and you should expect to reach the summit...with a much easier and quicker climb.

The right guides need to be an essential part of your climbing team.

Committed team

You'll recall how the leader of the British effort, John Hunt, "through his belief in teamwork, brought together a band of men who together would attempt this lofty peak," in the words of the British Royal Geographical Society.

1953 Everest Climbing Team & Guides

You read how a methodical team approach by the British Everest expedition allowed the final climbing pair of Edmund Hillary and Tenzing Norgay to reach the summit. From the organizational genius of team leader Hunt to the three-man support team of fellow climbers that accompanied Hillary and Norgay all but the final thousand feet or so, Hillary and Norgay reached the summit as the result of a team effort. Your success in the journey up the mountain of reinventing your agency requires a similar team effort.

So what does your climbing team look like? You certainly don't need 362 porters to carry your equipment up the slope, which should be a big relief to you.

What you do need – in addition to your expert guides – are a team of 10-15 peers: progressive, like-minded – preferably non-competitive – agency leaders who, like you, are fiercely committed to the climb and to the reinvention of their agency into a 21st Century Agency. You need 10-15 so that you get a broad enough group that they will have the range of experience and knowledge you need for your journey. The last thing you need at a critical juncture in your reinvention journey is to ask an important question of your team and get nothing but blank stares. You also want a large enough number to provide you with a powerful mastermind (I'll discuss that in a minute).

While your guides might come and go as needed, these men and women will be an integral part of your climb from Base Camp to the summit. As part of what we call an executive peer-exchange network, they can provide you three critical elements:

> Their own experience and agency best practices;

> Encouragement and moral support; and

> Accountability.

This team of agency leaders can provide the answer you need when you're stuck in a situation, the boost you need when you become discouraged, and the gift of accountability when you may be inclined to put off a challenging path in your journey to the top. Because these peers are making the same climb you are to reinvent their agency, they will understand your challenges, frustrations and impatience. And they will celebrate your successes and victories.

You need to be able to access the best thinking and experience of successful agency principals who have agreed to pop their hoods and give you full access to their operations and best practices. Some of them already will have attempted one or more of the strategies in this book; you want to be able to learn from both their mistakes and their successes. And since they are on the same journey with their own agency, they will be able to share tips and warnings, insights and shortcuts that can make your task a lot easier and save you valuable time. An executive peer-exchange network will provide you access to their invaluable counsel.

Mastermind

Out of purely selfish motives, you should bring these agency peers together into what is called a "mastermind" group, which would agree to meet regularly, either in person or, more likely, on conference calls. When collaborating as part of the mastermind group, you and your peers will be able to brainstorm ideas and strategies that can benefit every member of the group. The ability of a well-designed mastermind group to generate the right answer to a question and the solution to a problem is uncanny and almost eerie. As you begin your climb, you deserve – and need – to be able to harness the power of the mastermind. (See "What Is A MasterMind Group?" in the Appendix.)

Scouting your team

So where do you find your 10-15 team members? If you know local agency principals you trust, include them on your team if they are willing to commit to the agency reinvention enterprise. Beyond your competitors, check your Rolodex for principals you've met at conferences or carrier events. You might use LinkedIn as a resource and search for agency principals that you can contact and ask about their plans to reform proof their agency. And, of course, once you've found five or six peers who meet all the criteria, you can ask them to undertake the same search for principals in their network to reach the magic number of 10-15.

Jim Rohn reminds us, "You cannot succeed by yourself." Your peer-exchange team is your support network that will give you a leg up when you need it most and provide you with the wisdom, knowledge and experience that comes from living the same

Your own expedition to conquer the summit

A goal without a plan
is just a dream.
—Elbert Hubbard

20

Develop A Timeline for Your Climb
Setting Your Date to Summit

As you begin this climb up the mountain of agency reinvention to remain viable and thrive post reform, you must develop for yourself, your team and your agency a plan and timeline of achievement.

Proceeding without a written plan and timeline, would be like trying to summit a mountain like Everest without a detailed plan of ascension. You may have the right map, the right tools, and the right team but without a plan of attack, you have no reference as to how slow or fast you're moving toward your goal. The pace is just as critical as the direction.

Move too fast, and the quality of effort suffers. Move too slowly and the opportunity erodes out from under you.

Now, I can't suggest your timeline for success within the confines of this book. There are agency leaders at many different levels of current success and transformation. Instead, what I can and will do is provide you with a framework for developing your own plan of ascension up this daunting mountain from Base Camp all the way to Camp VI and on to the summit.

Reverse Engineering

In order to begin, we must know the end. Specifically, we must have an end date for when your agency will be reinvented. Yes, it will always be a work-in-progress but you need to determine a specific date to shoot for to achieve each milestone, to reach each camp along the journey.

Most agency leaders have given us Tuesday, January 2, 2014 as THE date. It's the first business day after the New Year. Of course, the reality is that the work must be done before then due to the holidays. I would also tell you that if you attempt this journey alone, without the proper help, without the proper tools, etc., reaching the summit of agency transformation on or before January 2, 2014 is very unlikely. That's not pessimism, that's realism.

Regardless, you must determine your end date. You must select the point in the future when you will arrive at the top of the mountain, looking down on all those who were unsuccessful in their endeavor as well as those who never even began, feeling admiration and empathy with the former and pity for the latter. You can register and commit to your date below.

On the following pages, I've outlined your journey, your ascension to the summit. I've given you the six key milestones or Camps that you must reach in order to successfully reach the top.

Below that, I've given lines to fill in for each Marker. On these lines write the smaller steps you must take, those achievements you must attain or create to reach the given Camp. These are like the checkpoints up the path of a mountain leading you to the summit. For you, they may be strategies to implement, team members to bring on, or small goals that must be achieved.

Finally, at the bottom of each page, there is a statement for you to complete by including a specific date you reach that camp, as well as a place for your firm's name, and your signature below committing yourself to this vital process and the overall journey.

Once you have achieved each Camp I through VI, you are ready to step onto the summit. You will have reached the top of the mountain and can celebrate your status as a 21st Century Agency.

TARGET SUMMIT DATE

To complete my climb to the reinvention of my business, I set the following date as my target for reaching the summit as a 21st Century Agency: _____

DATE

_____
SIGNATURE

CAMP I – An Expanded, Diversified Solutions Portfolio

Marker:

_____

_____

Marker:

_____

_____

Marker:

_____

_____

Marker:

_____

_____

Marker:

_____

_____

Marker:

_____

_____

Marker:

_____

_____

On _____, _____
    ACTUAL DATE   FIRM NAME

has reached Camp I, having created a 21st Century portfolio with an expanded and diversified toolbox of solutions.

_____
SIGNATURE

CAMP II – The High-ROI Marketing System Implemented

Marker:

_____

_____

Marker:

_____

_____

Marker:

_____

_____

Marker:

_____

_____

Marker:

_____

_____

Marker:

_____

_____

Marker:

_____

_____

On _____, _____

    ACTUAL DATE   FIRM NAME

has reached Camp II, having implemented 21st Century marketing by adopting the High-ROI Marketing System.

_____

SIGNATURE

CAMP III – The Advisory Selling Approach Adopted

Marker:
_____

_____

Marker:
_____

_____

Marker:
_____

_____

Marker:
_____

_____

Marker:
_____

_____

Marker:
_____

_____

Marker:
_____

_____

On _____, _____
    ACTUAL DATE   FIRM NAME

has reached Camp III, having trained its producers on 21st Century selling with the Advisory Selling system to be a consultative agency.

_____

SIGNATURE

CAMP IV – Maximum Results Produced Through Management

Marker: _____

_____

Marker: _____

_____

Marker: _____

_____

Marker: _____

_____

Marker: _____

_____

Marker: _____

_____

Marker: _____

_____

On _____, _____
ACTUAL DATE   FIRM NAME

has reached Camp IV, having implemented 21st Century management strategies to get maximum results from operations and producers.

_____

SIGNATURE

CAMP V – Prepared to Implement a Fee-for-Service Model

Marker: _____

_____

Marker: _____

_____

Marker: _____

_____

Marker: _____

_____

Marker: _____

_____

Marker: _____

_____

Marker: _____

_____

On _____, _____

ACTUAL DATE   FIRM NAME

has reached Camp V, being prepared and ready to move to a fee-for-service business model.

_____

SIGNATURE

CAMP VI – Completed Reevaluation of the Reinvention Process

Marker: _____

_____

Marker: _____

_____

Marker: _____

_____

Marker: _____

_____

Marker: _____

_____

Marker: _____

_____

Marker: _____

_____

On _____, _____
   ACTUAL DATE   FIRM NAME

has reached Camp VI, having completed a thorough re-evaluation of the reinvention process to confirm all aspect of a 21st Century Agency.

_____

SIGNATURE

I wish you absolute best as you begin this journey. It will not be easy, it will take time, and it WILL be worth it! I hope you grab your metaphorical backpack and climbing tools and find a highly motivated and committed team to join you as you summit to the mountaintop.

The climb to 29,000 feet begins with but one step.... Reading this book was that vital first step.

It's now time to take your next step.

When a gifted team dedicates itself to unselfish trust and combines instinct with boldness and effort, it is ready to climb.
—Patanjali

.

21

Your Next Step

Before you read another line, STOP and register your book at www.DOorDIEthebook.com**. Then you will have total access to the valuable resources and tools available to you online.**

This final chapter will be rather short. And to the point.

Your next step will determine whether or not you are successful in reinventing your business into a 21st Century Agency. And, thus, whether or not you and your agency will be one of the winners in the coming industry shakeout. So choose wisely.

As I see it, you have just four options of what to do.

Option 1   You can refuse to do. But expect to die as agency. Your time left is limited. But if you've gotten this far, I seriously doubt you will choose this fatal option.

Option 2   Using this book as your map, you can attempt to climb the mountain alone. I don't recommend it...you can still find Maurice Wilson's corpse on the side of Everest, far below the summit. But it's your agency and your future. There might be a couple of rare souls who can summit the mountain solo. (It was achieved finally on Everest but not until 1980 and only then by the man known as "the greatest climber in history.") Perhaps you are that exceptional one who can reinvent his agency with no help....

Option

3

Using the information in the two previous chapters, you can create your own expedition and, as the team leader, manage your climb the top:

> Research and assemble your team of agency principals for your peer network;

> Research and hire the expert guides whose expertise you'll need for your various reinvention tasks;

> If possible, identify and hire a mentor from among the experts you find;

> Form your mastermind group and arrange for regular meetings with your executive peers;

> Create the timeline for your climb with the appropriate checkpoints and camp milestones en route to reaching the summit on your determined end date;

> Work with your expert guides to implement the strategies and tactics in this book;

> Identify and secure from your guides the proper tools to make your climb easier and faster;

> Convene and facilitate the mastermind with your peers regularly for tips, shortcuts, answers, solutions, encouragement and accountability;

> Monitor your progress along your checkpoints to make sure you are on schedule;

> Use your experts to help you train your staff and producers to become competent with the new strategies;

> Celebrate your successes upon reaching Camp I, then Camp II, etc.;

> Upon reaching the top, review your milestone camps to ensure your new business model and systems are functioning properly; and, finally,

> Celebrate like hell for reaching the summit and contact me with the news. Congratulations will be in order!

That's a lot of work for you do but the prize – preserving your livelihood and your legacy – should be well worth the effort.

Option

4

You can get help to make your climb to reinvent your agency into a 21st Century Agency much easier and quicker – and almost certain to be successful.

If you are thinking right now, "I want help!" remember that in the Introduction I promised that I would show you how to get some serious help to make agency reinvention happen in your business more easily and quickly.

That mind-boggling TO DO list you just read in Option Three to create your expedition...

... we've done all that for you. All you have to do is just join our expedition to summit the mountain.

Look, after talking with a number of agency leaders and in the process of writing this book, Scott and I came to realize just how daunting a task this truly is. You are wanting to embark on a journey to completely reinvent your agency, after all. That's a damn steep mountain to climb.

We realize that this book is a fantastic start and gives you a trustworthy map to direct you up the mountain.

But no one wants to be Maurice Wilson.

Agency Success Mastermind Network

So we felt obligated to take the information in this book to the next level and create a unique turnkey program for agency leaders that parallels the British expeditionary force that conquered Everest and that will help you succeed in reinventing your agency into a 21st Century Agency.

Just like the book, however, this program is not for every agency leader. In fact, it's only for a small, elite group of serious, ambitious, open-minded and progressive agency leaders committed to making a successful journey up a very steep mountain.

In fact, your revenues may be too low to justify the investment required.

But you're still reading, so let me describe the Agency Success Mastermind Network...

Just *IMAGINE*...

...arriving at Base Camp on the first day of the program and meeting 10-15 of your peers – non-competing progressive agency leaders like you, who are driven, energized and committed to summiting this mountain– ready to take a 12-month journey with you up the mountain to reinvent their agency before 2014.

IMAGINE... gathering with your peers at three exclusive events held at luxury resorts and hotels across the country for intensive workshops and presentations from our industry's leading experts that will make your climb easier and faster.

IMAGINE... meeting face-to-face with these highly-motivated peers in professionally facilitated mastermind sessions (See Appendix for more information on the mastermind concept) at these events, discussing the tasks at hand, brainstorming, and sharing best practices and personal experiences with the reinvention process.

IMAGINE... continuing these dynamic and productive mastermind sessions every month on private conference calls for breakthrough ideas, encouragement and accountability.

IMAGINE... having complete and ongoing access to all the business-building information and insightful conversations through the transcripts and recordings of the mastermind calls & live sessions, workshops and presentations held at the events that you can refer back to for ideas and guidance as you make your climb.

IMAGINE... having direct access to the industry's top authority on consultative selling, cross-selling and voluntary benefits...

...to the industry's leading expert on insurance marketing and the use of direct response strategies to create high-ROI marketing...

...to one of the premier industry authorities on agency management, performance benchmarks, and agency valuation...

...to one of the top authorities on insurance sales management and benefits strategic planning...

...and to some of the most highly regarded experts on specialties such as time management, internet marketing, benefits communication, agency technology, public relations, and referrals.

IMAGINE... having some of the industry's top experts working one-on-one with you personally to mentor and guide you on your journey up the mountain.

IMAGINE... getting priceless tools and techniques handed to you by your expert guides to assist your climb.

IMAGINE... a customized 12-month timeline for your journey that will move you steadily from your Base Camp up through Camps I, II, III, IV, V and VI on your way to the summit – your agency now a 21st Century Agency, all in just 12 months.

IMAGINE... the immense sense of relief and power you will have knowing that your agency is reform proof and poised to dominate your market, all in time for the full implementation of PPACA on Thursday, January 2nd, 2014.

If you are interested in knowing more about the Agency Success Mastermind Network, here's your next step:

Go to www.21stCenturyAgency.com
and fill out a brief Interest Form.

You will be contacted by phone to discuss the program and your interest. If it seems like you and your agency are a potential fit for the program after the phone interview and we answer your questions to your satisfaction, we'll reserve your seat in the program for 48 hours to give you time to complete the Agency Mastermind Network Application that we'll send you. Once we receive your application, we'll process it and let you know if your agency has been accepted into the program.

Call our offices at (615) 656-5974
if you have questions.

Four options total.

Only **two options** that promise success in your ascent up the mountain to post-reform success as a 21st Century Agency.

Only **one option** that puts you in a turnkey program led and facilitated by leading industry experts that surrounds you with a group of excited and motivated executive peers in a process that will move you up the mountain and help you transform your agency into a reform-proof 21st Century Agency.

The choice is yours.

I wish you the best of luck on your climb to the summit and your 21st Century Agency.

I want to hear from you in a year or so...

"Well, Nelson, we knocked the bastard off."

Contact Information

To contact

Nelson Griswold or **Scott Cantrell...**

Email them:

info@InsuranceBottomLine.com

Call their office at Bottom Line Solutions:

(615) 656-5974

Visit the Bottom Line Solutions on the web:

www.InsuranceBottomLine.com

Appendix

Contents

What Is A Mastermind Group? 239

Learning to Speak "HR" 241

Cross-Selling Workplace Voluntary Benefits 243

Evaluation Checklist for WVB Enrollment Firms 259

Unique Selling Proposition (USP) Formula Cheat Sheet 261

Advisory Selling® Power Questions 263

The Art of Client (and Commission) Retention 267

The Prospect Quality Matrix 269

What Is A Mastermind Group?

So, what is a Mastermind group, exactly?

Mastermind groups offer a combination of brainstorming, education, peer accountability and support in a group setting to sharpen your business and personal skills. A Mastermind group helps you and your Mastermind group members achieve success. Participants challenge each other to set important goals, and more importantly, to accomplish them. The group requires commitment, confidentiality, and willingness to be creative and brainstorm ideas/solutions, and support each other with total honesty, respect and compassion. Mastermind group members act as catalysts for growth, devil's advocates and supportive colleagues. This is the essence and value of Mastermind groups.

What a Mastermind Group Is NOT

A MASTERMIND GROUP IS NOT A TRAINING CLASS. While groups can vote to bring in guest speakers occasionally to teach on a specific topic, the main focus of a Mastermind group is sharing among the group members.

A MASTERMIND GROUP IS NOT GROUP COACHING. Mastermind groups are about the MEMBERS' sharing with each other, not about the facilitator leading or coaching individuals in a group setting. You get EVERYONE'S feedback, advice and support.

A MASTERMIND GROUP IS NOT A NETWORKING AND REFERRAL GROUP. While you may share leads and resources with each other, the main focus of a Mastermind group is brainstorming and support to create success.

Napoleon Hill's Definition

The concept of the "Mastermind alliance" was formally introduced by Napoleon Hill in his timeless classic, *Think And Grow Rich*, though Mastermind groups have been around since the beginning of time.

Napoleon Hill wrote about the Mastermind group principle as: "The coordination of knowledge and effort of two or more people, who work toward a definite purpose, in the spirit of harmony."

He continues... "No two minds ever come together without thereby creating a third, invisible intangible force, which may be likened to a third mind [the master mind]."

What You'll Get from Belonging to a Mastermind Group

In a Mastermind group, the agenda belongs to the group and each person's participation and commitment is key. Your Mastermind partners give you feedback, help you brainstorm new possibilities, and set up accountability structures that keep you focused and on track. You create a community of supportive colleagues who brainstorm together to move the members to new heights. You'll gain tremendous insights, which improve your business and personal life. Your Mastermind group is like having an objective board of directors, an accountability group, a success team, and a peer advisory group, all rolled into one.

You Choose The Areas Where Your Mastermind Group Will Help You:

- ➢ Motivation
- ➢ Inspiration
- ➢ Goals
- ➢ Strategies
- ➢ Tactics
- ➢ Productivity
- ➢ Implementation
- ➢ Accountability

Learning to Speak "HR"

Resources to help you become conversant in the
issues and language of your HR clients.

ASSOCIATIONS

- **Society for Human Resource Management**
  www.shrm.org

  One word: JOIN. Not only will you become conversant in the language of HR, you'll be able to network with local HR professionals.

  With more than 190,000 individual members, the Society for Human Resource Management is the largest human resource management association in the world. The website offers information on local meetings, seminars and conferences.

WEBSITES

- **HR Executive Online**
  www.hronline.com

  News, Strategies and Resources for Senior HR Executives

- **Workforce Management**
  www.workforce.com

  The online home of *Workforce Management* magazine, a leading source of information and strategies for employee management for HR professionals.

PERIODICALS

- ***HR Magazine***
  www.shrm.org/Publications/hrmagazine

  As the flagship publication for SHRM, *HR Magazine* is the premier source for HR knowledge including leadership development; labor relations; new strategies for healthcare; compensation and retirement security; and global organizational change. *HR Magazine* is the publication to which HR professionals turn to find the most innovative HR practices and solutions. ($70 annual subscription; Free with SHRM membership)

- ***Workforce Management***
  www.workforce.com

  Workforce Management magazine highlights the current issues facing HR professionals.

- ***Employee Benefit News***

  www.benefitnews.com

  Employee Benefit News is the benefit industry's leading magazine for HR professionals.

E-NEWSLETTERS

- ***HR Week***

  www.shrm.org/Publications/E-mailNewsletters

  HR Week offers a weekly roundup of HR news, issues affecting the profession and additions to the SHRM web site. With more than 300,000 subscribers, *HR Week* is one of the leading periodicals for the HR profession.

- ***HRE Online Update***

  http://www.hreonline.com/HRE/newsletters.jsp

  A summary of the latest print and online editions of Human Resource Executive®, the leading source of news, strategies and resources for senior HR executives.

  NOTE: The following three e-newsletters require (free) registration on workforce.com. Once registered, subscribe by using the E-Newsletters section on the left hand side of the page.

- ***Workforce Week***

  http://www.workforce.com

  A concise, useful newsletter with quick links to articles, time-saving tools, and HR news.

- ***Workforce Benefits***

  http://www.workforce.com

  Timely and insightful news, trends and in-depth information on the world of benefits.

- ***Dear Workforce***

  http://www.workforce.com

  An occasionally eye-opening question-and-answer newsletter addressing some of the most common and most obscure HR dilemmas.

Cross-Selling Workplace Voluntary Benefits

A Short Cut to Advisory Selling and the Single Most Effective
Strategy for Replacing Lost Medical Commissions!

By Nelson L. Griswold

MetLife's 2011 broker and consultant study reveals that, faced with
serious concerns about medical commission cuts and maintaining top-line
revenues, fully 58 percent of brokers and consultants are embracing two
specific initiatives:

- Becoming more consultative; and
- Cross-selling more voluntary product.

The excellent news is that there is a very simple way to become consultative
AND cross-sell voluntary effectively – at the same time with the same process.

Cross-selling WVB the right way – the way that consistently sells cases
and puts premium on the books – is inherently a consultative process that
puts you on the same side of the table with your client and solves difficult
HR-related problems for the client.

If you want to become more consultative and you want an easy-to-
implement process, cross-selling voluntary benefits the right way will make
you more consultative.

If you want to sell voluntary and you want the process to be natural and
successful, you must take a consultative approach to your clients.

In the Broker Boot Camp® training events on cross-selling voluntary that
I conduct across the country for carriers and agencies, I show brokers how to
use a consultative approach to cross-sell voluntary. After the Boot Camp,
most of the brokers tell me this is the first exposure to consultative selling
they've ever had.

Any producer will become more consultative by cross-selling voluntary
benefits the right way with this easy-to-implement four-step process.

Broker resistance

A cover story in a leading insurance industry publication proclaimed:
"Everyone says they're doing it. But these guys really are."[16] The headline

---

[16] Denis Storey, "Voluntary Crusader," *Benefits Selling* June 2007: cover.

referred to cross-selling worksite voluntary benefits and one broker's bold steps in this area.

But what of the unspoken implication of the headline? Despite strong incentives and the best intentions of some, the overwhelming majority of benefits brokers were *not* cross-selling voluntary benefits. And five years later, most of them still aren't.

Why? Why are brokers not cross-selling voluntary benefits even when:

> ➤ Commissions on major medical plans continue to decrease due to market and regulatory pressures;

> ➤ Voluntary benefits continue to be one of the industry's fastest growing product segments;

> ➤ Voluntary benefits provide a substantial, new revenue source that can help replace declining commissions from major medical;

> ➤ Cross-selling existing clients is about 60 percent less expensive than developing new business;

> ➤ The Aflac and Colonial sales armies are hammering continuously on their clients' door to put in voluntary benefits;

> ➤ Employees "ask for it at work" thanks to Aflac's persistent, high-profile advertising campaign; and

> ➤ Agency leadership in small shops to the regional and national houses are encouraging producers to cross-sell voluntary.

Despite the fact that WVB has been around for over 50 years and today is a more than $6 billion industry, most benefits brokers resist cross-selling these very lucrative products. Why?

Based on conversations with hundreds of brokers, I've discovered the overwhelming top two reasons brokers don't cross-sell WVB:

1) IGNORANCE

Brokers simply don't understand the voluntary products, the WVB sales or enrollment process, and, most important, the value proposition of selling WVB—both to the broker and to HR. This isn't stupidity; you can't fix stupid. This is just a lack of familiarity and understanding and *that* we can fix.

2) FEAR

A broker's greatest fear is losing the account. Enrolling WVB is a relatively complex process compared to core benefits, requiring one-on-one enrollment meetings at the worksite. Brokers fear that the process will damage the client relationship and cost the BOR. But a well-managed WVB enrollment will protect the account while generating substantial commission revenue.

Also, brokers fear having to do more work. Because of the complexity, there is work involved. But, in most cases, the broker doesn't have to take on additional work.

We'll look at how brokers can avoid the dangers and extra work of a voluntary enrollment later in this piece.

The cross-sell fail

Some brokers attempt to cross-sell WVB but fail repeatedly, finally deciding that worksite voluntary just can't be sold.

The single reason most brokers fail in cross-selling voluntary benefits is that they push product. They make the WVB sale to the employer all about products.

Yet most employers don't want to hear about more products for their employees. The employer does want to hear about how the broker can make their jobs easier! And voluntary benefits can help brokers do that, solving pressing employer problems at no cost to the employer.

All voluntary benefits are not created equal

The Number One mistake brokers make about worksite voluntary benefits is confusing group voluntary, such as dental and vision, with worksite voluntary benefits like critical illness, accident and permanent life.

The key differences are that worksite offers employees **much more valuable benefits** that pay the agency's choice of high, front-loaded commissions or robust level commissions. Either way, the financial payout isn't even comparable to group voluntary plans.

Show me the money!

Most brokers have no idea of just how lucrative worksite voluntary benefits can be. The following formulae allow a broker to calculate the revenue potential of a single voluntary benefits case, or an entire book of business.

Large case: For cases over 100 lives, the broker must partner with an enrollment firm to enroll the employees.

The enrollment firm will do almost all of the heavy lifting, from case set up to wrap up, leaving the broker free to open new accounts. The broker pays the enrollment firm with a split of the WVB commission.

The large case commission formula reflects a standard 65/35 split of the commission, with the broker getting the 35 percent. Here's the formula for calculating **net commission** to the broker using a heaped commission schedule when an enrollment firm is involved:

$58 x number of eligible employees

That's $5,800 net to the broker for a 100-life group, with no extra work!

Small case: For groups under 100 lives, the broker may want to enroll the case himself or with a colleague or friend. (For most brokers, I don't advise this. The retail sale of WVB to an employee is specialized and an entirely different sale than selling benefits to an employer. Plus, it's important to factor in the opportunity cost when the broker could be out opening new accounts.) But in those instances where the broker does enroll the case and she knows how to sell the WVB to the employee, here's the formula for calculating **net commission** (not premium) to the broker:

$104 x number of eligible employees

On just a 25-life group the broker nets $2,600!

Do the math with your own book & see just how lucrative worksite WVB can be to your business. There simply is no substitute for replacing lost medical commissions.

Enrollment help

Let me emphasize again that brokers should always partner with a benefits enrollment firm to enroll groups with more than 100 employees in voluntary benefits, unless the agency has a trained voluntary enrollment team in house. Enrollment firms specialize in the project management and benefit communication in face-to-face enrollment meetings that are essential to a successful enrollment that satisfies the employer & puts premium on the books.

For managing and enrolling the case, the broker splits the WVB commission with the enrollment partner, with the enrollment firm's split ranging from 60-75 percent.

But it's my money!

A lot of brokers balk at giving up such a large portion of what they see as "their" commission.

Since experience has proven that successful voluntary enrollments require the specialized expertise of these enrollment firms, it's important for brokers to understand splits with enrollment firms.

The enrollment firm doesn't just bring essential expertise that very few brokers possess. The enrollment partner will do 95 percent of the heavy lifting on a case, freeing you to focus on bringing in new business and helping you avoid the opportunity costs of having to enroll the voluntary.

Enrollments are expensive, labor-intensive projects because of the need for benefit counselors (enrollers) to meet individually with every employee. Voluntary benefits do not sell themselves; these products must be presented to employees by trained benefit counselors in order to get good participation and write meaningful premium.

The best enrollment firms do not use commissioned benefit counselors; they pay a daily fee plus expenses.

The enrollment firm accepts responsibility for all costs of enrollment. So, for the broker, the enrollment is all upside, with no chance of losing money. If the enrollment goes south and little premium is written, the enrollment firm can lose tens of thousands of dollars, mostly in enroller fees.

Enrollment costs typically are 15 to 20 percent of gross commissions. These direct enrollment costs (fees & travel expenses for case managers and benefit counselors) are factored into the split percentage.

The net result of the commission split between the broker and the enrollment firm should be to produce, *after expenses*, a 50-50 split of the commission between the two.

In other words, the broker splits the profits evenly with the enrollment partner in exchange for the enrollment firm doing all the project management work and putting the premium on the books to produce the commission. The broker gets half the profit for bringing the case, the enrollment firm gets half for doing all the work. Explained this way, almost all brokers see the fairness in that deal.

Protect your accounts

Client retention is all the more important to brokers in this economy and with declining commissions. Yet brokers face challenges from more than just other benefit brokers looking to grab their BOR.

There are three business-stealing threats that brokers keep out of their accounts by cross-selling voluntary benefits. Although both Aflac and Colonial do work through brokers, these are voluntary carriers with massive field forces that write employers direct. While these carriers don't threaten the medical, brokers have to contend with an Aflac or Colonial rep messing around in *their* account.

Also, clever benefits brokers have learned to avoid a frontal assault on the medical BOR by coming in the back door by bringing voluntary benefits into an account where the broker of record hasn't offered WVB. Once in the account with the voluntary, it's only a matter of time before that broker is quoting against the in-force broker on the medical.

Finally, payroll companies like ADP and Paychex that have employee benefits divisions are offering their payroll clients voluntary benefits as a way to introduce their benefits business and back door the broker of record. By virtue of controlling the payroll and by offering an integrated software solution for benefit administration and open enrollment, these companies are making a strong move to take over brokers' accounts.

The brilliant Chinese military strategist Sun Tzu advised:

What is of supreme importance is to attack the enemy's strategy.

Cross-selling WVB into accounts **now** will slam that back door shut and lock in clients.

Take control of your client relationships

Many benefits brokers I know live in fear of their clients. It's understandable, really. The employer determines whether the broker continues to get the commission whether he keeps the account. And for too many health brokers, their value to the client is no greater than their latest renewal offer.

The power dynamic greatly favors the employer. The broker brings a health plan that the client can get from most any other broker while the client represents to the broker a sizable commission on the medical. No wonder brokers lay awake at night worried about losing their accounts.

A fantastic result of cross-selling WVB the right way is that you begin to take control of the broker/client relationship. How? By solving problems for the client, you start to provide more value to the client than the client brings you. By becoming a problem solver, you raise your value to the client far beyond the renewal price. In fact, price (in this case, the renewal) becomes a very secondary consideration for the client!

Additionally, by using voluntary benefits to solve problems for the client, you lock in the account, since problem solvers are hard to come by. As a problem solver, you become the clients trusted advisor. What client is going to get rid of a broker like that?!

By now, most brokers are convinced that worksite voluntary benefits are good business and a powerful way to take the power position in their broker/client relationships. But some, especially older brokers, balk at selling what they consider substandard, low-value WVB products.

What's in WVB for employees

Today's voluntary benefits aren't your grandfather's cancer plan. In the past, there *were* some shoddy WVB products that didn't provide much value to employees.

Today's WVB products are high-quality, high-value products from blue-chip carriers and valuable life and health plans that meet the needs and fit the lifestyles of today's employees..

No longer do one-size-fits-all benefit plans serve the needs of our diverse workforce. Young and old, singles and families, employees have different needs based on their stage in the life cycle. When offered a range of voluntary benefits, employees are empowered to create their ideal benefit plan.

In a well-planned worksite enrollment supported by HR, participation in a new voluntary offering can reach 50-60 percent or more of eligible employees. Voluntary benefits do not sell themselves; but when trained benefit counselors explain these benefits to employees, employees want these benefits because they understand their value and want the financial protection they offer.

Moreover, WVB help fill the gaps in an employee benefit plan. Every benefit plan has gaps – such as the large out-of-pocket exposure with a high-deductible medical plan or the six months before the LTD plan kicks in – that employees will want to fill with voluntary benefits. WVB is an affordable and easy way for employers to expand their benefit options and accommodate their employees' needs.

The leading worksite voluntary benefits are, in no particular order:

- Permanent life insurance
- Short term disability
- Accident
- Critical illness
- Cancer
- Hospital Indemnity

Plus, employees want (and need) the financial security offered by voluntary benefits. With today's economic and job insecurity, these products give employees more control over their benefits and make them less dependant on their employer for their financial security.

Finally, payroll deduction makes these valuable benefits affordable to working-class employees.

Once brokers understand the value of cross-selling WVB and the value of these benefits to employees, they're ready to cross-sell voluntary to their clients. But most brokers who try to cross-sell WVB aren't successful.

Why brokers fail at cross-selling

The first thing to know is that the value proposition of voluntary benefits is different for HR than for employees.

For employees, the value of WVB is in the actual benefits.

For the employer, the primary value of worksite voluntary is in the *solutions* provided by both the benefits and the ancillary services available in the enrollment process.

The number one reason most brokers fail cross-selling voluntary benefits:

Pushing product.

Too many producers make the worksite voluntary sale a product sale.

The reality is very few HR departments want to hear about more benefits for their employees. Many will complain that their employees don't use the benefits they already have. Many will state that their employees don't want, don't need, and/or can't afford the voluntary benefits...before even learning what the products are and how much they cost! That's a hard argument to win and one best avoided.

They may not want more products for the benefits plan but HR *does* want solutions to their problems. Using worksite WVB the producer can provide HR with *solutions* – not just products – and eliminate HR's pain – not just "make a sale." The broker can solve pressing HR issues at no cost to the client. That always gets their attention!

Cross-selling WVB to the employer

The biggest mistake brokers make in cross-selling worksite voluntary benefits is to make it a product sale.

The number one secret of top producers to cross-selling voluntary benefits to employers:

Use WVB & the enrollment process to solve problems for the employer.

Employers rarely are looking for new benefits for their plan but they *are* eager for solutions to their most critical problems.

Sometimes, the benefits themselves can be the solution. As employee-paid benefits, WVB can freshen the benefits plan at no cost to the employer. They're also ideal for filling gaps in the core plan, such as the 180-day elimination period in the long-term disability plan that can be covered by a voluntary six-month short-term disability plan.

And WVB provides employers what I call "*positive* cost shifting." Instead of the usual premium increase for the same benefits or a reduced benefit for the same premium, voluntary benefits give employees a choice of benefits they can elect based on their specific needs to increase their financial protection.

The value of the WVB enrollment

I wrote in the chapter on Portfolio that one of the least-understood aspects of voluntary benefits is just how valuable a WVB enrollment can be to employers. Most brokers just don't realize that the associated services, not the benefits themselves, are the key to selling the employer on a WVB offering.

In order to sell these benefits to employees, it's necessary for a trained benefit counselor who understands their value proposition to present the benefits to employees in one-on-one enrollment meetings.

This process of a voluntary benefit enrollment can solve a number of important HR-related problems.

Here are some key results that WVB and the enrollment process can deliver for employers:

> **Enhanced employee benefits at no cost to the employer**

  The employer can offer employees valuable new benefits that don't add to the benefits budget.

> **Improved open enrollment process**

  This can include improved benefit communication, the elimination of paper applications, and electronic transfer of the enrollment data to carriers.

> **Increased plan participation**

  A WVB enrollment can boost participation in all products, including high-deductible medical plans/HSA/HRA, FSA and 401(k) plans.

> **Benefit education & communication**

Benefit counselors can communicate the benefit plan to employees one-one-one far more effectively than a group meeting, benefit booklet or website.

> **Improved employee morale and retention**

When employees understand their benefit plan, their appreciation for their benefits improves employee morale, reducing turnover.

> **Reduced open enrollment burden on HR**

The benefit enrollment firm will free up the HR staff by handling most of the logistics and organization of OE.

Here are some other valuable solutions that WVB can provide, usually at no cost, primarily for mid-market employers with 250 or more employees:

> **Dependent eligibility audits**, which can save the client huge sums by ensuring that only eligible dependents are on the medical plan; and

> **Benefit administration software**, which provides online enrollment and can help HR manage their benefit plan.

> **Online self-service onboarding**, which fully automates the process to provide a comprehensive and compliant new-hire orientation and benefits enrollment provided by an avatar virtual communicator.

NOTE: Most of these services are provided by the enrollment firm as part of their value proposition. The selection of an enrollment partner must be guided in part by its service offerings.

Funding mechanism

Cross-selling WVB is about solving a problem for the client with either the benefits or the enrollment. Offering the voluntary benefits now becomes a means to an end: It pays for the solution that the employer desperately wants.

After all, nothing is free. Every solution has to be paid for.

The secret is to sell the solution to the client and then show how the solution is paid for by the commissions on the WVB.

One powerful tip

This powerful tip will transform your relationship with your HR client:

Enter the HR conversation. Your HR clients actually spend only a small portion of their time on insurance issues. The HR world encompasses many other areas. Since WVB can solve problems in some of these areas, learn what they are.

Learn to speak HR, not just insurance, and enter the HR conversation with your clients.

Overcoming the fear factor

Even if he understands the voluntary products and process, a broker's fear of a WVB enrollment can cause him to avoid voluntary. Finding the right strategic partners is the most effective antidote to the fear factor holding back producers from cross-selling voluntary benefits.

Producers who resist cross-selling voluntary out of fear are right about one thing: Done badly, a voluntary enrollment can be a nightmare for the client and can cost the producer the BOR letter. So, too, can billing problems with the voluntary.

But so can a high renewal on the medical plan and billing and/or claims issues with the supplemental term life or LTD benefits.

Ours is an industry that depends on getting the details right: the right plan design, carrier, and rate negotiation for the major medical plan...the right plan design and carrier(s) for the supplemental benefits...an effective and well-managed open enrollment.

The same is equally true for the voluntary benefits side of the business. The first requirement is to recognize and evaluate the actual risks posed by WVB.

Acknowledging the Risks

There *are* real risks to a worksite enrollment, primarily:

➤ Botched enrollment;

➤ Low participation; and

➤ Billing and claims problems.

Brokers can manage the risk by selecting the right carrier & managing the enrollment correctly.

Let's take a look at each of the three risks and best practice strategies to manage them.

RISK Botched enrollments

First, botched enrollments occur because the enrollment isn't managed by an experienced case manager. An enrollment isn't complicated but it is complex with a lot of moving parts. Either the broker or agency staff must manage the case internally if it's a small group (under 100 lives) or otherwise hire a professional enrollment firm. While an enrollment firm should always be used for large-group enrollments, small group cases pose a very real challenge to an agency.

Managing an enrollment

For small groups, best practice is for a broker to use a carrier that offers small-group enrollment services. Or, if the broker has built a professional enrollment capability within the firm, he can manage the case himself and enroll employees personally, use agency staff that have been specially trained, or hire a professional licensed benefit counselor.

For the broker that wants to manage the case himself, there are some important facts to understand.

There are a lot of moving parts involved but an enrollment essentially has only two components:

1) Project management

2) Benefit communication (selling)

WVB must be presented to employees by trained benefit counselors in mandatory one-on-one meetings at the workplace, ideally preceded (but not replaced) by group meetings. For larger employee groups dispersed across a large number of small locations or where face-to-face meeting are not possible, there are two workable alternatives:

- A call center
- Self-service online enrollment but only if using a *virtual benefit counselor* (avatar) to replace the onsite benefit counselor.

Please note that employee interaction with the call center or online virtual benefit counselor must be *mandatory* to ensure acceptable participation.

There are three enrollment roles:

1) **Enrollment Manager** – Oversees case setup with the carrier and employer, schedules the enrollment, and handles pre-enrollment communication of the WVB

2) **Case Manager** – Manages the onsite enrollment; often a veteran benefit counselor

3) **Benefit Counselor** (enroller) – Licensed agent who communicates the WVB to employees & enrolls them

For cases under 100, the broker often plays all three roles or sometimes delegates the enrollment to licensed staff or a contract benefit counselor.

Any enrollment has ten main components:

1) **Product Selection** – What products meet client needs

2) **Getting Good Working Conditions** (Access to Employees) – Mandatory one-on-one enrollment meetings with employees

3) **Enrollment Strategy** – How best to enroll the employees

4) **Case Setup** – Facilitating the billing call with employer & carrier, managing enrollment dates & logistics, and managing client expectations

5) **Pre-enrollment Communication** – Communicating the offering to employees before the enrollment

6) **Benefit Counselor Training** – Ensuring mastery of the voluntary plans as well as the client's core benefits (if communicating the core benefits during OE)

7) **Managing Onsite Enrollment Logistics** – Ensuring the enrollment is on schedule and without problems

8) **Enrolling "Stragglers"** – Enrolling eligible employees who are unavailable during the enrollment

9) **Enrollment Evaluation** – Reviewing with the employer what went right and what can be improved for next year's enrollment

10) **Re-enrollment Strategy** – Gaining agreement from the employer for changes to next year's enrollment conditions that will increase participation & premium, possibly to include offering a new voluntary benefit

Again, WVB enrollments are not complicated but they do have some complexity and risks that must be acknowledged & managed. With the information above, any broker is well equipped to manage the risks and ensure a successful and profitable WVB enrollment.

RISK Low participation

Low participation is a huge risk. Why? Two primary reasons.

First, however the case is sold to the employer, the broker must assure the client that the employees will want the WVB being offered. When participation is low, the client is left to assume that the broker is either ignorant or a liar. Neither conclusion favors the broker.

Second, with no participation, there's nothing in it for any of the parties involved. Low participation means the employees don't get the financial protection the benefits provide and the broker gets no meaningful commission revenue. With no comp, why make the effort to cross-sell WVB in the first place?

Low participation almost always is a function of either poor access to the employees or poorly trained benefit counselors. Benefit counselors well trained in presenting WVB to employees in a consultative fashion are essential to good participation. Without good access to employees in the form of one-on-one enrollment meetings, however, not even the very best benefits counselors can generate participation and put premium on the books.

The broker must insist on good access to employees as key to a successful WVB enrollment...for the employer, employees and the broker. For larger groups, a strong enrollment firm partner can both assist with HR to obtain good working conditions and provide highly trained benefit counselors to ensure high participation in the voluntary.

Picking the right enrollment partner

For the producer who wants to cross-sell voluntary benefits, the key detail to get right is the selection of his or her enrollment partner. The right benefit communication and enrollment firm will do 90 percent of the work on each voluntary case. Both the operational success of the enrollment and the revenue generated depend on the expertise of the enrollment firm. The right enrollment partner is essential to getting the right employee access, effectively communicating the offering to employees, and dependably managing the project.

While a growing number of companies offer worksite enrollment services, mid-size to large brokers need to decide carefully on a strategic enrollment partner with the right characteristics and capabilities.

`RISK` Billing and claims problems

Billing and claims are the provinces of the carrier. While there is almost never any service work for the agency on voluntary claims, billing problems can and do happen.

While the enrollment is over after a few days or weeks at the most, billing is forever and poses a serious risk for the broker. This makes the selection of the voluntary benefits carrier a very important decision.

Picking the right voluntary carrier partner

The broker's challenge is to choose a carrier partner from those carriers with solid portfolios that can service what they sell.

There are six key criteria to choosing the right carrier (in *ascending* order of importance; last is most important):

6) **Broker Compensation** – A competitive commission schedule is key. But remember that high commissions won't make up for billing or claims headaches in the future. Also, some carriers will give the broker a choice of level or heaped commissions.

5) **Product** – While most WVB carriers offer similar product, some do offer best-of-breed in a category. More important is *breadth of portfolio*; look for a full range of WVB products, so you can meet your client's needs now and still offer new products in ensuing years without having to bring in a new carrier.

4) **Enrollment Support** – Whether you enroll the case yourself or use an enrollment firm, carrier support for case setup is critical. Enrollment technology – the software used on laptops to enroll employees – should be user-friendly and reliable.

3) **Value-added Services** – This is any additional service that a carrier might offer. For example, one carrier offers consolidated billing for all WVB products, even those from other carriers. That same carrier offers wellness programs at no cost to the client in exchange for offering their voluntary. Others offer a discount on the major medical for placing their WVB in the account. Some carriers offer a discount on the Stop Loss premium for offering their Critical Illness.

2) **Experience with Voluntary Benefits** – With so many new carriers entering the WVB space, be sure that your carrier partner has committed the resources to support the voluntary in the ways covered in these criteria.

1) **Back Office** – The most critical consideration is the carrier's ability to support the WVB sold into your account. Claims handling affects the employees, while billing impacts the employer. Problems with either can cost you the account.

With how it handles claims & billing, the carrier determines the long-term success of the voluntary offering.

The right voluntary carrier will offer not only quality benefits at competitive rates but also have a back office capable of supporting the products fully. Not all voluntary carriers are created equal. There are many carriers jumping into the voluntary benefits space; only a handful boasts a credible back office operation that can provide dependable billing and service claims efficiently. Choosing the right carrier is essential to ensuring the long-term satisfaction of both employees and HR.

Besides choosing the carrier for the strength of its back office, brokers should match their carrier partner to the client's needs, so that the products and or services suit the client's requirements.

While your relationship with the enrollment firm on a WVB case is more like a date, you're marrying the carrier. Choose wisely.

Not only can WVB add needed new revenues to an agency, it provides additional Velcro® between the broker and his clients, boosting retention and strengthening the broker/client relationship.

And cross-selling voluntary benefits the right way helps to make the producer consultative with clients. Two birds, one stone.

Evaluation Checklist for
Voluntary Benefits Enrollment Firms

This checklist should be completed for each voluntary benefits case, basing the evaluation on the client's specific needs and case requirements.

These criteria are in ascending order, with the least important first and ending with the most important.

ENROLLMENT FIRM: _____

- ❏ Commission split _____% to the broker
- ❏ Services & technology
  - ❏ Call center (if needed)
  - ❏ Ancillary services (if needed)
  - ❏ Enrollment technology (if needed)
- ❏ Benefit counselors
  - ❏ Training
  - ❏ Per diem compensation
- ❏ Capacity
  - ❏ Case size
  - ❏ Enrollment type
  - ❏ Geographical range
- ❏ Re-enrollment strategy (Multi-year)
- ❏ Infrastructure
  - ❏ Expertise
  - ❏ Management
  - ❏ Support staff
- ❏ Track record
  - ❏ Business experience
  - ❏ Carrier experience
  - ❏ Case results

Unique Selling Proposition (USP) Formula Cheat Sheet

By Scott Cantrell

Your most important marketing tool is your unique selling proposition (USP).

Your USP is a statement of your business's most significant benefit and point of differentiation to your target market. Simply put, it's the reason why a prospect would do business with you and not someone else.

Follow these six simple steps, and you'll have a powerful marketing tool in your arsenal.

STEP 1 First, know your target market and write down everything you can about them and what you would want if you were them. Put yourself in their shoes. Make a list of the benefits you would want from an agency like yours.

STEP 2 Next, write down everything about your service or product you can think of. How does it benefit your clients? How does your product or service work?

STEP 3 Third, you want to create your resume if you will. Write down all the things about yourself that make you/your product qualified to solve the prospects' problems.

STEP 4 Take all these lists and information and look through them. You are looking for specific aspects of yourself and your business that benefit your clients that your competition does not have or is not telling his clients about. Yes, you may have to research your competition to see what specifically is different between you and them.

STEP 5 Now, begin to write a statement or paragraph including all those great benefits for your clients. Be sure to include a couple of points about your service or product to create credibility around it and your business. Once you've got several written, read them all, combine them, add to and subtract from and edit the material until you think you've got the perfect USP.

STEP 6 Finally, try it out. Let your friends read it and promote it to your clients through your promotional materials (i.e. flyers, website, business card, etc.) and see how people react to it. If people specifically mention something positive about it or recall your USP, then you know you've got a winner!

USP Template

For the past (Number of Years in Business), more than (Number of Clients Helped) have been (Verb of Benefit - i.e. 'protected') by (Your Name or Agency Name), through (Differentiation of Process) to produce (Biggest Client Benefits).

Advisory Selling® Power Questions

By Nelson L. Griswold

RAPPORT & PRIORITY QUESTIONS

Use these questions to develop greater rapport with your clients and to better understand them and their priorities for their department.

- Why did you get into human resources (HR)?

- What activities or initiatives do you most enjoy about your job?

- What HR activities or initiatives are most important to you?

- Of all the HR functions and activities, what are the most important to employees?

- What are your top three priorities for your department?

- What would you like to accomplish that you haven't already?"

- If you had a bigger budget, what would be your spending priorities?

"DISCOVERY" QUESTIONS Identify the Client's Pain Points

Use these questions to identify those problems that cause your client the most pain and discomfort.

NOTE: When executing the pain questions you will sometimes need to use nurturing statements to soften the impact of some of your deep exploratory questions. For example:

- *"Do you mind if I ask..."*
- *"I'm not sure if this is applicable..."*
- *"Can I ask you a personal question?"*
- *"I'm a little awkward asking you this..."*

Continue asking discovery questions until you identify a problem (pain point) that you can solve with voluntary benefits or the services of a voluntary benefits enrollment.

- Other than managing health care costs, what are your most pressing problems?

- What work-related issues cause you to lose sleep at night?

- What work activities are the most frustrating?

- What activities consume the most staff time?

- What are the most hated parts of your job?

- What are the biggest needs in your department?

- What HR or benefits issues most concern company management?

- If you could change anything in your department, what would it be?

- What would make your department more efficient and/or effective?

- If you could spend 15-20 minutes with each employee, what would you talk about?

"PAIN" QUESTIONS Agitate the Client's Pain

This is the critical step, where you create the demand for the solution you are going to bring the client. Once you've identified a problem of your client's that you can solve with voluntary benefits or the services of a VB enrollment, use these pain questions to drill down into that problem and agitate the client's pain around the problem.

If you do your job properly with these questions, *asked with persistence but also with empathy and understanding*, your client almost will be squirming recalling the unpleasantness and pain caused by the problem. This isn't sadism. Your goal is to help your client remember just how badly she needs a solution. *Your* solution.

NOTE: Not all of these questions will pertain to every problem. Obviously, ask only those questions that apply to the problem at hand.

- **Why is the problem such a problem?**
  What are the symptoms and consequences of the problem?

- **What are the most difficult aspects of the problem?**
  Find out the crux of the problem, the most painful issues.

- **How long has the problem existed?**
  Is this a temporary situation or an ongoing challenge?

- **What will happen if the problem continues?**
  Short and long term ramifications should be explored

- **What has been done thus far to address the problem?**
  This answer could be your "door opener" later!

- **What were the results of those efforts to "fix" the problem?**
  Actions taken and money spent should be quantified here.

- **What is the cost thus far of this problem?**
  Here you can determine what it cost them NOT to solve their problem.

- **Are there budgeted funds available to "fix" this problem?**
  If there aren't, why not and will there be? Either way, do you have a deal for them!

- **How much staff time does the problem take up?**
  Discover the "soft cost" of the problem, which leads into the next question.

- **What activities would you prefer to be doing if you weren't tied down by the problem?**
  What are the opportunity costs of the problem?

"CONCEPTUAL AGREEMENT" Get the Prospect's Buy-In on the Solution

Once your pain questions have made the client sufficiently uncomfortable – but before you offer a solution – get conceptual agreement that a solution to the problem would be desirable.

- **So, if we could find a way to <eliminate the problem> (e.g., get your open enrollment off paper), that would be a good thing? Would that make your job easier?**

- **Would you be more productive if we could find a way to <eliminate the problem>?**

CLOSE QUESTIONS Get a "Yes"

Once you get conceptual agreement, offer a solution then ask your closing question.

- **Do you want to solve this problem today?**

- **Are you ready to get started now solving this problem?**

The Art of
Client (and Commission) Retention
A 10-Step Action Guide

By Scott Cantrell

STEP 1   Understand The Six Reasons Clients Don't Renew

1) They don't trust the broker.
2) They don't like the broker.
3) They aren't protected from the broker's competitors.
4) They aren't happy with the products & services, esp. price.
5) Their buying decision has not been validated.
6) They believe they no longer want or need the product or service.

STEP 2   Develop 'Client Service' Where You Preempt Problems Rather Than React To Them

STEP 3   Understand The Three Goals Of Consistent Communication

1) Control the Client Relationship
2) Care for the Client's Needs
3) Cross-Sell Relevant Products & Services to the Client

STEP 4   Design A 12-Month Contact Retention Plan

STEP 5   Write & Develop Each of the 68 Contacts & Communications
(Contact Scott for a Short-Cut)

STEP 6   Send Weekly Emails to Your Client List

STEP 7   Send Out A Monthly Mailing to Your Client List

STEP 8   Personally Call Each Client Every Three Months

STEP 9   Count The Extra Commissions You Brought In With Retained Business & Referrals!

STEP 10   Repeat Steps 1 to 9

The Prospect Quality Matrix
Focus On Your Firm's Highest Quality Prospects

By Scott Cantrell

The matrix below will guide your firm to identifying and focusing on the highest quality prospects – the ones you would most like to have as long-term clients. Notice that the horizontal axis measures how 'ideal' a prospect is for your business. That is, how much a particular prospect matches up with the specific demographic information of your most desired clients. The vertical axis measures the strength of the relationship between your business and the prospect in the meaningful terms of the Advisory Selling process.

Thus, four quadrants are created into which we can place any potential client. By consciously determining the quadrant that a given prospect is currently in, you can choose what needs to be done (if anything can be done) to move them into the upper right quadrant. Let me offer up an explanation of each quadrant in turn...

The Prospect Quality Matrix

No Opportunity – When there is no meaningful relationship and the prospect does not possess the qualities you want in a client, there is simply no real opportunity to work with them. Therefore, you should not waste time, money or manpower with them through your marketing or selling efforts.

Wasted Prospects – A prospect that does have the characteristics your firm is looking for in a potential client but who is not properly engaged with your firm and does not have a good relationship creates a wasted prospect and thus, a wasted opportunity. Anytime you identify a prospect with those ideal demographic qualities, the next step should always be focused on building a meaningful relationship with the prospect via the Advisory Selling process.

Just Friends – Most of us have our own, "let's just be friends" story from middle school. This is the result when we spend time and effort on a prospect that never really met the criteria for a good client. While you should not actively work to convert these prospects into clients, they can still become valuable advocates and referral sources.

Valuable, Long-Term Clients – When both elements (relationship and client demographics) come together, you'll have found a new ideal client for your benefits firm. Thus, these are the types of prospects you should focus on most. Focus on building meaningful relationships with those clients that match your specified criteria for an ideal client.

Finally, you'll note in the center of the matrix, a small oval of "Possible Prospects." Naturally, there are prospects that may not clearly be in one of the quadrants. As you identify those prospects, you'll have to use your best judgment to decide how many resources should be used to attempt to turn them into clients.